I0170829

DICTIONARY
THEME-BASED

ENGLISH-
HEBREW

The most useful words
To expand your lexicon and sharpen
your language skills

3000 words

Theme-based dictionary British English-Hebrew - 3000 words

By Andrey Taranov

T&P Books vocabularies are intended for helping you learn, memorize and review foreign words. The dictionary is divided into themes, covering all major spheres of everyday activities, business, science, culture, etc.

The process of learning words using T&P Books' theme-based dictionaries gives you the following advantages:

- Correctly grouped source information predetermines success at subsequent stages of word memorization
- Availability of words derived from the same root allowing memorization of word units (rather than separate words)
- Small units of words facilitate the process of establishing associative links needed for consolidation of vocabulary
- Level of language knowledge can be estimated by the number of learned words

·

T&P Books Publishing
www.tpbooks.com

This book is also available in E-book formats.
Please visit www.tpbooks.com or the major online bookstores.

HEBREW THEME-BASED DICTIONARY
British English collection

T&P Books vocabularies are intended to help you learn, memorize, and review foreign words. The vocabulary contains over 3000 commonly used words arranged thematically.

- Vocabulary contains the most commonly used words
- Recommended as an addition to any language course
- Meets the needs of beginners and advanced learners of foreign languages
- Convenient for daily use, revision sessions, and self-testing activities
- Allows you to assess your vocabulary

Special features of the vocabulary

- Words are organized according to their meaning, not alphabetically
- Words are presented in three columns to facilitate the reviewing and self-testing processes
- Words in groups are divided into small blocks to facilitate the learning process
- The vocabulary offers a convenient and simple transcription of each foreign word

The vocabulary has 101 topics including:

Basic Concepts, Numbers, Colors, Months, Seasons, Units of Measurement, Clothing & Accessories, Food & Nutrition, Restaurant, Family Members, Relatives, Character, Feelings, Emotions, Diseases, City, Town, Sightseeing, Shopping, Money, House, Home, Office, Working in the Office, Import & Export, Marketing, Job Search, Sports, Education, Computer, Internet, Tools, Nature, Countries, Nationalities and more ...

TABLE OF CONTENTS

PRONUNCIATION GUIDE

Letter's name	Letter	Hebrew example	T&P phonetic alphabet	English example
Alef	א	אריה	[ɑ], [ɑ:]	bath, to pass
	א	אחד	[ɛ], [ɛ:]	habit, bad
	א	מָאָה	['] (hamza)	glottal stop
Bet	ב	בית	[b]	baby, book
Gimel	ג	גמל	[g]	game, gold
Gimel+geresh	ג'	ג'ונגל	[dʒ]	joke, general
Dalet	ד	דג	[d]	day, doctor
Hei	ה	הר	[h]	home, have
Vav	ו	וסת	[v]	very, river
Zayin	ז	זאב	[z]	zebra, please
Zayin+geresh	ז'	ז'ורנל	[ʒ]	forge, pleasure
Chet	ח	חוט	[x]	as in Scots 'loch'
Tet	ט	טוב	[t]	tourist, trip
Yud	י	יום	[j]	yes, New York
Kaph	ך כ	בריש	[k]	clock, kiss
Lamed	ל	לחם	[l]	lace, people
Mem	ם מ	מלך	[m]	magic, milk
Nun	ן נ	נר	[n]	name, normal
Samech	ס	סוס	[s]	city, boss
Ayin	ע	עין	[ɑ], [ɑ:]	bath, to pass
	ע	תשעים	['] (ayn)	voiced pharyngeal fricative
Pei	ף פ	פיל	[p]	pencil, private
Tsadi	ץ צ	צעצוע	[ts]	cats, tsetse fly
Tsadi+geresh	צ'ץ'	צ'ק	[tʃ]	church, French
Qoph	ק	קוף	[k]	clock, kiss
Resh	ר	רכבת	[r]	French (guttural) R
Shin	ש	שלחן, עשרים	[s], [ʃ]	city, machine
Tav	ת	תפוז	[t]	tourist, trip

ABBREVIATIONS
used in the dictionary

English abbreviations

ab.	-	about
adj	-	adjective
adv	-	adverb
anim.	-	animate
as adj	-	attributive noun used as adjective
e.g.	-	for example
etc.	-	et cetera
fam.	-	familiar
fem.	-	feminine
form.	-	formal
inanim.	-	inanimate
masc.	-	masculine
math	-	mathematics
mil.	-	military
n	-	noun
pl	-	plural
pron.	-	pronoun
sb	-	somebody
sing.	-	singular
sth	-	something
v aux	-	auxiliary verb
vi	-	intransitive verb
vi, vt	-	intransitive, transitive verb
vt	-	transitive verb

Hebrew abbreviations

ז	-	masculine
ז"ר	-	masculine plural
ז, נ	-	masculine, feminine
נ	-	feminine
נ"ר	-	feminine plural

BASIC CONCEPTS

1. Pronouns

I, me	ani	אֲנִי (ז, נ)
you (masc.)	ata	אַתָּה (ז)
you (fem.)	at	אַתְּ (נ)
he	hu	הוּא (ז)
she	hi	הִיא (נ)
we	a'naxnu	אֲנַחְנוּ (ז, נ)
you (masc.)	atem	אַתֶּם (ז"ר)
you (fem.)	aten	אַתֶּן (נ"ר)
you (polite, sing.)	ata, at	אַתָּה (ז), אַתְּ (נ)
you (polite, pl)	atem, aten	אַתֶּם (ז"ר), אַתֶּן (נ"ר)
they (masc.)	hem	הֵם (ז"ר)
they (fem.)	hen	הֵן (נ"ר)

2. Greetings. Salutations

Hello! (fam.)	ʃalom!	שָׁלוֹם!
Hello! (form.)	ʃalom!	שָׁלוֹם!
Good morning!	'boker tov!	בּוֹקֶר טוֹב!
Good afternoon!	tsaha'rayim tovim!	צָהֳרַיִם טוֹבִים!
Good evening!	'erev tov!	עֶרֶב טוֹב!
to say hello	lomar ʃalom	לוֹמַר שָׁלוֹם
Hi! (hello)	hai!	הַיי!
greeting (n)	ahlan	אַהְלָן
to greet (vt)	lomar ʃalom	לוֹמַר שָׁלוֹם
How are you? (form.)	ma ʃlomex?, ma ʃlomxa?	מָה שְׁלוֹמֵךְ? (נ), מָה שְׁלוֹמְךָ? (ז)
How are you? (fam.)	ma niʃma?	מָה נִשְׁמַע?
What's new?	ma xadaʃ?	מָה חָדָשׁ?
Bye-Bye! Goodbye!	lehitra'ot!	לְהִתְרָאוֹת!
Bye!	bai!	בַּיי!
See you soon!	lehitra'ot bekarov!	לְהִתְרָאוֹת בְּקָרוֹב!
Farewell!	heye ʃalom!	הֱיֵה שָׁלוֹם!
Farewell! (form.)	lehitra'ot!	לְהִתְרָאוֹת!
to say goodbye	lomar lehitra'ot	לוֹמַר לְהִתְרָאוֹת
Cheers!	bai!	בַּיי!
Thank you! Cheers!	toda!	תּוֹדָה!
Thank you very much!	toda raba!	תּוֹדָה רַבָּה!
My pleasure!	bevakaʃa	בְּבַקָּשָׁה
Don't mention it!	al lo davar	עַל לֹא דָּבָר
It was nothing	ein be'ad ma	אֵין בְּעַד מָה

Excuse me!	sliẋa!	סליחה!
to excuse (forgive)	lis'loaẋ	לסלוח
to apologize (vi)	lehitnatsel	לְהִתְנַצֵּל
My apologies	ani mitnatsel, ani mitna'tselet	אֲנִי מִתְנַצֵּל (ז), אֲנִי מִתְנַצֶּלֶת (נ)
I'm sorry!	ani mitsta'er, ani mitsta''eret	אֲנִי מִצְטַעֵר (ז), אֲנִי מִצְטַעֶרֶת (נ)
to forgive (vt)	lis'loaẋ	לסלוח
It's okay! (that's all right)	lo nora	לא נוֹרָא
please (adv)	bevakaʃa	בְּבַקָשָׁה
Don't forget!	al tiʃkaẋ!	אַל תִשְׁכַּח! (ז)
Certainly!	'betaẋ!	בֶּטַח!
Of course not!	'betaẋ ʃelo!	בֶּטַח שֶלֹא!
Okay! (I agree)	okei!	אוֹקֵיי!
That's enough!	maspik!	מַסְפִּיק!

3. Questions

Who?	mi?	מִי?
What?	ma?	מָה?
Where? (at, in)	'eifo?	אֵיפֹה?
Where (to)?	le'an?	לְאָן?
From where?	me''eifo?	מֵאֵיפֹה?
When?	matai?	מָתַי?
Why? (What for?)	'lama?	לָמָה?
Why? (~ are you crying?)	ma'du'a?	מַדוּעַ?
What for?	biʃvil ma?	בִּשְׁבִיל מָה?
How? (in what way)	eiẋ, keitsad?	כֵּיצַד? אֵיךְ?
What? (What kind of ...?)	'eize?	אֵיזֶה?
Which?	'eize?	אֵיזֶה?
To whom?	lemi?	לְמִי?
About whom?	al mi?	עַל מִי?
About what?	al ma?	עַל מָה?
With whom?	im mi?	עַם מִי?
How many? How much?	'kama?	כַּמָה?
Whose?	ʃel mi?	שֶל מִי?

4. Prepositions

with (accompanied by)	im	עַם
without	bli, lelo	בְּלִי, לְלֹא
to (indicating direction)	le...	לְ...
about (talking ~ ...)	al	עַל
before (in time)	lifnei	לִפְנֵי
in front of ...	lifnei	לִפְנֵי
under (beneath, below)	mi'taẋat le...	מִתַחַת לְ...
above (over)	me'al	מֵעַל
on (atop)	al	עַל

from (off, out of)	mi, me	מִ, מְ
of (made from)	mi, me	מִ, מְ
in (e.g. ~ ten minutes)	toχ	תוֹךְ
over (across the top of)	'dereχ	דֶּרֶךְ

5. Function words. Adverbs. Part 1

Where? (at, in)	'eifo?	אֵיפֹה?
here (adv)	po, kan	פֹּה, כָּאן
there (adv)	ʃam	שָׁם
somewhere (to be)	'eifo ʃehu	אֵיפֹה שֶׁהוּא
nowhere (not in any place)	beʃum makom	בְּשׁוּם מָקוֹם
by (near, beside)	leyad …	לְיַד ...
by the window	leyad haχalon	לְיַד הַחַלּוֹן
Where (to)?	le'an?	לְאָן?
here (e.g. come ~!)	'hena, lekan	הֵנָה; לְכָאן
there (e.g. to go ~)	leʃam	לְשָׁם
from here (adv)	mikan	מִכָּאן
from there (adv)	miʃam	מִשָּׁם
close (adv)	karov	קָרוֹב
far (adv)	raχok	רָחוֹק
near (e.g. ~ Paris)	leyad	לְיַד
nearby (adv)	karov	קָרוֹב
not far (adv)	lo raχok	לֹא רָחוֹק
left (adj)	smali	שְׂמָאלִי
on the left	mismol	מִשְּׂמֹאל
to the left	'smola	שְׂמֹאלָה
right (adj)	yemani	יְמָנִי
on the right	miyamin	מִיָּמִין
to the right	ya'mina	יָמִינָה
in front (adv)	mika'dima	מִקָּדִימָה
front (as adj)	kidmi	קִדְמִי
ahead (the kids ran ~)	ka'dima	קָדִימָה
behind (adv)	me'aχor	מֵאָחוֹר
from behind	me'aχor	מֵאָחוֹר
back (towards the rear)	a'χora	אָחוֹרָה
middle	'emtsa	אֶמְצַע (ז)
in the middle	ba''emtsa	בָּאֶמְצַע
at the side	mehatsad	מֵהַצַּד
everywhere (adv)	beχol makom	בְּכָל מָקוֹם
around (in all directions)	misaviv	מִסָּבִיב
from inside	mibifnim	מִבִּפְנִים

somewhere (to go)	le'an ʃehu	לְאָן שֶׁהוּא
straight (directly)	yaʃar	יָשָׁר
back (e.g. come ~)	baχazara	בַּחֲזָרָה
from anywhere	me'ei ʃam	מֵאֵי שָׁם
from somewhere	me'ei ʃam	מֵאֵי שָׁם
firstly (adv)	reʃit	רֵאשִׁית
secondly (adv)	ʃenit	שֵׁנִית
thirdly (adv)	ʃliʃit	שְׁלִישִׁית
suddenly (adv)	pit'om	פִּתְאוֹם
at first (in the beginning)	behatslaχa	בַּהַתְחָלָה
for the first time	lariʃona	לָרִאשׁוֹנָה
long before …	zman rav lifnei …	זְמַן רַב לִפְנֵי …
anew (over again)	meχadaʃ	מֵחָדָשׁ
for good (adv)	letamid	לְתָמִיד
never (adv)	af 'pa'am, me'olam	מֵעוֹלָם, אַף פַּעַם
again (adv)	ʃuv	שׁוּב
now (at present)	axʃav, ka'et	עַכְשָׁיו, כָּעֵת
often (adv)	le'itim krovot	לְעִיתִים קְרוֹבוֹת
then (adv)	az	אָז
urgently (quickly)	bidχifut	בִּדְחִיפוּת
usually (adv)	be'dereχ klal	בְּדֶרֶךְ כְּלָל
by the way, …	'dereχ 'agav	דֶּרֶךְ אַגַּב
possibly	efʃari	אֶפְשָׁרִי
probably (adv)	kanir'e	כַּנִּרְאָה
maybe (adv)	ulai	אוּלַי
besides …	χuts mize …	חוּץ מִזֶּה …
that's why …	laχen	לָכֵן
in spite of …	lamrot …	לַמְרוֹת …
thanks to …	hodot le…	הוֹדוֹת לְ…
what (pron.)	ma	מָה
that (conj.)	ʃe	שֶׁ
something	'maʃehu	מַשֶּׁהוּ
anything (something)	'maʃehu	מַשֶּׁהוּ
nothing	klum	כְּלוּם
who (pron.)	mi	מִי
someone	'miʃehu, 'miʃehi	מִישֶׁהוּ (ז), מִישֶׁהִי (נ)
somebody	'miʃehu, 'miʃehi	מִישֶׁהוּ (ז), מִישֶׁהִי (נ)
nobody	af eχad, af aχat	אַף אֶחָד (ז), אַף אַחַת (נ)
nowhere (a voyage to ~)	leʃum makom	לְשׁוּם מָקוֹם
nobody's	lo ʃayaχ le'af eχad	לֹא שַׁיָּךְ לְאַף אֶחָד
somebody's	ʃel 'miʃehu	שֶׁל מִישֶׁהוּ
so (I'm ~ glad)	kol kaχ	כָּל־כָּךְ
also (as well)	gam	גַּם
too (as well)	gam	גַּם

6. Function words. Adverbs. Part 2

Why?	ma'du'a?	מַדּוּעַ?
for some reason	miʃum ma	מִשּׁוּם־מָה
because ...	miʃum ʃe	מִשּׁוּם שֶׁ
for some purpose	lematara 'kolʃehi	לְמַטָרָה כָּלְשֶׁהִי
and	ve ...	וְ ...
or	o	אוֹ
but	aval, ulam	אֲבָל, אוּלָם
for (e.g. ~ me)	biʃvil	בִּשְׁבִיל
too (excessively)	yoter midai	יוֹתֵר מִדַי
only (exclusively)	rak	רַק
exactly (adv)	bediyuk	בְּדִיּוּק
about (more or less)	be''ereχ	בְּעֵרֶךְ
approximately (adv)	be''ereχ	בְּעֵרֶךְ
approximate (adj)	meʃo'ar	מְשׁוֹעָר
almost (adv)	kim'at	כִּמְעַט
the rest	ʃe'ar	שְׁאָר (ז)
the other (second)	aχer	אַחֵר
other (different)	aχer	אַחֵר
each (adj)	kol	כֹּל
any (no matter which)	kolʃehu	כָּלְשֶׁהוּ
many, much (a lot of)	harbe	הַרְבֵּה
many people	harbe	הַרְבֵּה
all (everyone)	kulam	כּוּלָם
in return for ...	tmurat ...	תְּמוּרַת ...
in exchange (adv)	bitmura	בִּתְמוּרָה
by hand (made)	bayad	בַּיָד
hardly (negative opinion)	safek im	סָפֵק אִם
probably (adv)	karov levadai	קָרוֹב לְוַודַּאי
on purpose (intentionally)	'davka	דַּווְקָא
by accident (adv)	bemikre	בְּמִקְרֶה
very (adv)	me'od	מְאוֹד
for example (adv)	lemaʃal	לְמָשָׁל
between	bein	בֵּין
among	be'kerev	בְּקֶרֶב
so much (such a lot)	kol kaχ harbe	כָּל־כָּךְ הַרְבֵּה
especially (adv)	bimyuχad	בִּמְיוּחָד

NUMBERS. MISCELLANEOUS

7. Cardinal numbers. Part 1

0 zero	'efes	אֶפֶס (ז)
1 one	exad	אֶחָד (ז)
1 one (fem.)	axat	אַחַת (נ)
2 two	'ʃtayim	שְׁתַּיִם (נ)
3 three	ʃaloʃ	שָׁלוֹשׁ (נ)
4 four	arba	אַרְבַּע (נ)
5 five	xameʃ	חָמֵשׁ (נ)
6 six	ʃeʃ	שֵׁשׁ (נ)
7 seven	'ʃeva	שֶׁבַע (נ)
8 eight	'ʃmone	שְׁמוֹנֶה (נ)
9 nine	'teʃa	תֵּשַׁע (נ)
10 ten	'eser	עֶשֶׂר (נ)
11 eleven	axat esre	אַחַת-עֶשְׂרֵה (נ)
12 twelve	ʃteim esre	שְׁתֵּים-עֶשְׂרֵה (נ)
13 thirteen	ʃloʃ esre	שְׁלוֹשׁ-עֶשְׂרֵה (נ)
14 fourteen	arba esre	אַרְבַּע-עֶשְׂרֵה (נ)
15 fifteen	xameʃ esre	חָמֵשׁ-עֶשְׂרֵה (נ)
16 sixteen	ʃeʃ esre	שֵׁשׁ-עֶשְׂרֵה (נ)
17 seventeen	ʃva esre	שְׁבַע-עֶשְׂרֵה (נ)
18 eighteen	ʃmone esre	שְׁמוֹנֶה-עֶשְׂרֵה (נ)
19 nineteen	tʃa esre	תְּשַׁע-עֶשְׂרֵה (נ)
20 twenty	esrim	עֶשְׂרִים
21 twenty-one	esrim ve'exad	עֶשְׂרִים וְאֶחָד
22 twenty-two	esrim u'ʃnayim	עֶשְׂרִים וּשְׁנַיִם
23 twenty-three	esrim uʃloʃa	עֶשְׂרִים וּשְׁלוֹשָׁה
30 thirty	ʃloʃim	שְׁלוֹשִׁים
31 thirty-one	ʃloʃim ve'exad	שְׁלוֹשִׁים וְאֶחָד
32 thirty-two	ʃloʃim u'ʃnayim	שְׁלוֹשִׁים וּשְׁנַיִם
33 thirty-three	ʃloʃim uʃloʃa	שְׁלוֹשִׁים וּשְׁלוֹשָׁה
40 forty	arba'im	אַרְבָּעִים
41 forty-one	arba'im ve'exad	אַרְבָּעִים וְאֶחָד
42 forty-two	arba'im u'ʃnayim	אַרְבָּעִים וּשְׁנַיִם
43 forty-three	arba'im uʃloʃa	אַרְבָּעִים וּשְׁלוֹשָׁה
50 fifty	xamiʃim	חֲמִישִׁים
51 fifty-one	xamiʃim ve'exad	חֲמִישִׁים וְאֶחָד
52 fifty-two	xamiʃim u'ʃnayim	חֲמִישִׁים וּשְׁנַיִם
53 fifty-three	xamiʃim uʃloʃa	חֲמִישִׁים וּשְׁלוֹשָׁה
60 sixty	ʃiʃim	שִׁישִׁים
61 sixty-one	ʃiʃim ve'exad	שִׁישִׁים וְאֶחָד

62 sixty-two	ʃiʃim u'ʃnayim	שִׁישִׁים וּשְׁנַיִים
63 sixty-three	ʃiʃim uʃloʃa	שִׁישִׁים וּשְׁלוֹשָׁה
70 seventy	ʃiv'im	שִׁבְעִים
71 seventy-one	ʃiv'im ve'eχad	שִׁבְעִים וְאֶחָד
72 seventy-two	ʃiv'im u'ʃnayim	שִׁבְעִים וּשְׁנַיִים
73 seventy-three	ʃiv'im uʃloʃa	שִׁבְעִים וּשְׁלוֹשָׁה
80 eighty	ʃmonim	שְׁמוֹנִים
81 eighty-one	ʃmonim ve'eχad	שְׁמוֹנִים וְאֶחָד
82 eighty-two	ʃmonim u'ʃnayim	שְׁמוֹנִים וּשְׁנַיִים
83 eighty-three	ʃmonim uʃloʃa	שְׁמוֹנִים וּשְׁלוֹשָׁה
90 ninety	tiʃ'im	תִּשְׁעִים
91 ninety-one	tiʃ'im ve'eχad	תִּשְׁעִים וְאֶחָד
92 ninety-two	tiʃ'im u'ʃayim	תִּשְׁעִים וּשְׁנַיִים
93 ninety-three	tiʃ'im uʃloʃa	תִּשְׁעִים וּשְׁלוֹשָׁה

8. Cardinal numbers. Part 2

100 one hundred	'me'a	מֵאָה (נ)
200 two hundred	ma'tayim	מָאתַיִים
300 three hundred	ʃloʃ me'ot	שְׁלוֹשׁ מֵאוֹת (נ)
400 four hundred	arba me'ot	אַרְבַּע מֵאוֹת (נ)
500 five hundred	χameʃ me'ot	חָמֵשׁ מֵאוֹת (נ)
600 six hundred	ʃeʃ me'ot	שֵׁשׁ מֵאוֹת (נ)
700 seven hundred	ʃva me'ot	שְׁבַע מֵאוֹת (נ)
800 eight hundred	ʃmone me'ot	שְׁמוֹנֶה מֵאוֹת (נ)
900 nine hundred	tʃa me'ot	תְּשַׁע מֵאוֹת (נ)
1000 one thousand	'elef	אֶלֶף (ז)
2000 two thousand	al'payim	אַלְפַּיִים (ז)
3000 three thousand	'ʃloʃet alafim	שְׁלוֹשֶׁת אֲלָפִים (ז)
10000 ten thousand	a'seret alafim	עֲשֶׂרֶת אֲלָפִים (ז)
one hundred thousand	'me'a 'elef	מֵאָה אֶלֶף (ז)
million	milyon	מִילְיוֹן (ז)
billion	milyard	מִילְיַארְד (ז)

9. Ordinal numbers

first (adj)	riʃon	רִאשׁוֹן
second (adj)	ʃeni	שֵׁנִי
third (adj)	ʃliʃi	שְׁלִישִׁי
fourth (adj)	revi'i	רְבִיעִי
fifth (adj)	χamiʃi	חֲמִישִׁי
sixth (adj)	ʃiʃi	שִׁישִׁי
seventh (adj)	ʃvi'i	שְׁבִיעִי
eighth (adj)	ʃmini	שְׁמִינִי
ninth (adj)	tʃi'i	תְּשִׁיעִי
tenth (adj)	asiri	עֲשִׂירִי

COLORS. UNITS OF MEASUREMENT

10. Colours

colour	'tseva	צֶבַע (ז)
shade (tint)	gavan	גָּוֶן (ז)
hue	gavan	גָּוֶן (ז)
rainbow	'keʃet	קֶשֶׁת (נ)
white (adj)	lavan	לָבָן
black (adj)	ʃaχor	שָׁחוֹר
grey (adj)	afor	אָפוֹר
green (adj)	yarok	יָרוֹק
yellow (adj)	tsahov	צָהוֹב
red (adj)	adom	אָדוֹם
blue (adj)	kaχol	כָּחוֹל
light blue (adj)	taχol	תְּכוֹל
pink (adj)	varod	וָרוֹד
orange (adj)	katom	כָּתוֹם
violet (adj)	segol	סָגוֹל
brown (adj)	χum	חוּם
golden (adj)	zahov	זָהוֹב
silvery (adj)	kasuf	כָּסוּף
beige (adj)	beʒ	בֶּז'
cream (adj)	be'tseva krem	בְּצֶבַע קְרֶם
turquoise (adj)	turkiz	טוּרְקִיז
cherry red (adj)	bordo	בּוֹרְדוֹ
lilac (adj)	segol	סָגוֹל
crimson (adj)	patol	פָּטוֹל
light (adj)	bahir	בָּהִיר
dark (adj)	kehe	כֵּהֶה
bright, vivid (adj)	bohek	בּוֹהֵק
coloured (pencils)	tsiv'oni	צִבְעוֹנִי
colour (e.g. ~ film)	tsiv'oni	צִבְעוֹנִי
black-and-white (adj)	ʃaχor lavan	שָׁחוֹר-לָבָן
plain (one-coloured)	χad tsiv'i	חַד-צִבְעִי
multicoloured (adj)	sasgoni	סַסְגּוֹנִי

11. Units of measurement

weight	miʃkal	מִשְׁקָל (ז)
length	'oreχ	אוֹרֶךְ (ז)

width	'roχav	רוֹחַב (ז)
height	'gova	גוֹבַה (ז)
depth	'omek	עוֹמֶק (ז)
volume	'nefaχ	נֶפַח (ז)
area	'ʃetaχ	שֶׁטַח (ז)

gram	gram	גרָם (ז)
milligram	mili'gram	מִילִיגרָם (ז)
kilogram	kilo'gram	קִילוֹגרָם (ז)
ton	ton	טוֹן (ז)
pound	'pa'und	פָּאוּנד (ז)
ounce	'unkiya	אוּנקִיָּה (נ)

metre	'meter	מֶטֶר (ז)
millimetre	mili'meter	מִילִימֶטֶר (ז)
centimetre	senti'meter	סַנטִימֶטֶר (ז)
kilometre	kilo'meter	קִילוֹמֶטֶר (ז)
mile	mail	מַייל (ז)

inch	intʃ	אִינץ' (ז)
foot	'regel	רֶגֶל (נ)
yard	yard	יַרד (ז)

| square metre | 'meter ra'vu'a | מֶטֶר רָבוּעַ (ז) |
| hectare | hektar | הֶקטָר (ז) |

litre	litr	לִיטר (ז)
degree	ma'ala	מַעֲלָה (נ)
volt	volt	ווֹלט (ז)
ampere	amper	אַמפֵּר (ז)
horsepower	'koaχ sus	כּוֹחַ סוּס (ז)

quantity	kamut	כַּמוּת (נ)
a little bit of …	ktsat …	קצָת ...
half	'χetsi	חֲצִי (ז)
dozen	tresar	תרֵיסָר (ז)
piece (item)	yeχida	יְחִידָה (נ)

| size | 'godel | גוֹדֶל (ז) |
| scale (map ~) | kne mida | קנֵה מִידָה (ז) |

minimal (adj)	mini'mali	מִינִימָאלִי
the smallest (adj)	hakatan beyoter	הַקָּטָן בְּיוֹתֵר
medium (adj)	memutsa	מְמוּצָע
maximal (adj)	maksi'mali	מַקסִימָלִי
the largest (adj)	hagadol beyoter	הַגָּדוֹל בְּיוֹתֵר

12. Containers

canning jar (glass ~)	tsin'tsenet	צְנצֶנֶת (נ)
tin, can	paχit	פַּחִית (נ)
bucket	dli	דלִי (ז)
barrel	χavit	חָבִית (נ)
wash basin (e.g., plastic ~)	gigit	גִיגִית (נ)

tank (100L water ~)	meiẋal	מֵיכָל (ז)
hip flask	meimiya	מֵימִייָה (נ)
jerrycan	'dʒerikan	גֵ'רִיקָן (ז)
tank (e.g., tank car)	meẋalit	מֵיכָלִית (נ)
mug	'sefel	סֵפֶל (ז)
cup (of coffee, etc.)	'sefel	סֵפֶל (ז)
saucer	taẋtit	תַחְתִית (נ)
glass (tumbler)	kos	כּוֹס (נ)
wine glass	ga'vi°a	גָבִיעַ (ז)
stock pot (soup pot)	sir	סִיר (ז)
bottle (~ of wine)	bakbuk	בַּקְבּוּק (ז)
neck (of the bottle, etc.)	tsavar habakbuk	צַוָואר הַבַּקְבּוּק (ז)
carafe (decanter)	kad	כַּד (ז)
pitcher	kankan	קַנְקַן (ז)
vessel (container)	kli	כְּלִי (ז)
pot (crock, stoneware ~)	sir 'ẋeres	סִיר חֶרֶס (ז)
vase	agartal	אֲגַרְטָל (ז)
flacon, bottle (perfume ~)	tsloẋit	צלוֹחִית (נ)
vial, small bottle	bakbukon	בַּקְבּוּקוֹן (ז)
tube (of toothpaste)	ʃfo'feret	שפוֹפֶרֶת (נ)
sack (bag)	sak	שָׂק (ז)
bag (paper ~, plastic ~)	sakit	שָׂקִית (נ)
packet (of cigarettes, etc.)	ẋafisa	חֲפִיסָה (נ)
box (e.g. shoebox)	kufsa	קוּפְסָה (נ)
crate	argaz	אַרְגָז (ז)
basket	sal	סַל (ז)

MAIN VERBS

to advise (vt)	leya'ets	לְיַיעֵץ
to agree (say yes)	lehaskim	לְהַסכִּים
to answer (vi, vt)	la'anot	לַעֲנוֹת
to apologize (vi)	lehitnatsel	לְהִתנַצֵל
to arrive (vi)	leha'gi'a	לְהַגִיע
to ask (~ oneself)	liʃol	לִשאוֹל
to ask (~ sb to do sth)	levakeʃ	לְבַקֵש
to be (vi)	lihyot	לִהיוֹת
to be afraid	lefaχed	לְפַחֵד
to be hungry	lihyot ra'ev	לִהיוֹת רָעֵב
to be interested in ...	lehit'anyen be...	...בְּ לְהִתעַניֵין
to be needed	lehidareʃ	לְהִידָרֵש
to be surprised	lehitpale	לְהִתפַּלֵא
to be thirsty	lihyot tsame	לִהיוֹת צָמֵא
to begin (vt)	lehatχil	לְהַתחִיל
to belong to ...	lehiʃtayeχ	לְהִשתַייֵך
to boast (vi)	lehitravrev	לְהִתרַברֵב
to break (split into pieces)	liʃbor	לִשבּוֹר
to call (~ for help)	likro	לִקרוֹא
can (v aux)	yaχol	יָכוֹל
to catch (vt)	litfos	לִתפּוֹס
to change (vt)	leʃanot	לְשַנוֹת
to choose (select)	livχor	לִבחוֹר
to come down (the stairs)	la'redet	לָרֶדֶת
to compare (vt)	lehaʃvot	לְהַשווֹת
to complain (vi, vt)	lehitlonen	לְהִתלוֹנֵן
to confuse (mix up)	lehitbalbel	לְהִתבַּלבֵּל
to continue (vt)	lehamʃiχ	לְהַמשִיך
to control (vt)	liʃlot	לִשלוֹט
to cook (dinner)	levaʃel	לְבַשֵל
to cost (vt)	la'alot	לַעֲלוֹת
to count (add up)	lispor	לִספּוֹר
to count on ...	lismoχ al	לִסמוֹך עַל
to create (vt)	litsor	לִיצוֹר
to cry (weep)	livkot	לִבכּוֹת

| to deceive (vi, vt) | leramot | לְרַמוֹת |
| to decorate (tree, street) | lekaʃet | לְקַשֵט |

to defend (a country, etc.)	lehagen	לְהָגֵן
to demand (request firmly)	lidroʃ	לִדרוֹש
to dig (vt)	laxpor	לַחפּוֹר

to discuss (vt)	ladun	לָדוּן
to do (vt)	la'asot	לַעֲשׂוֹת
to doubt (have doubts)	lefakpek	לְפַקפֵּק
to drop (let fall)	lehapil	לְהַפִּיל
to enter (room, house, etc.)	lehikanes	לְהִיכָּנֵס

to excuse (forgive)	lis'loax	לִסלוֹחַ
to exist (vi)	lehitkayem	לְהִתקַייֵם
to expect (foresee)	laxazot	לַחֲזוֹת
to explain (vt)	lehasbir	לְהַסבִּיר
to fall (vi)	lipol	לִיפּוֹל

to fancy (vt)	limtso xen be'ei'nayim	לִמצוֹא חֵן בְּעֵינַיים
to find (vt)	limtso	לִמצוֹא
to finish (vt)	lesayem	לְסַייֵם
to fly (vi)	la'uf	לָעוּף
to follow ... (come after)	la'akov axarei	לַעֲקוֹב אַחֲרֵי

to forget (vi, vt)	liʃ'koax	לִשכּוֹחַ
to forgive (vt)	lis'loax	לִסלוֹחַ
to give (vt)	latet	לָתֵת
to give a hint	lirmoz	לִרמוֹז
to go (on foot)	la'lexet	לָלֶכֶת

to go for a swim	lehitraxets	לְהִתרַחֵץ
to go out (for dinner, etc.)	latset	לָצֵאת
to guess (the answer)	lenaxeʃ	לְנַחֵש

to have (vt)	lehaxzik	לְהַחזִיק
to have breakfast	le'exol aruxat 'boker	לֶאֱכוֹל אֲרוּחַת בּוֹקֶר
to have dinner	le'exol aruxat 'erev	לֶאֱכוֹל אֲרוּחַת עֶרֶב
to have lunch	le'exol aruxat tsaha'rayim	לֶאֱכוֹל אֲרוּחַת צָהֳרַיים
to hear (vt)	liʃ'mo'a	לִשמוֹעַ

to help (vt)	la'azor	לַעֲזוֹר
to hide (vt)	lehastir	לְהַסתִּיר
to hope (vi, vt)	lekavot	לְקוּוֹת
to hunt (vi, vt)	latsud	לָצוּד
to hurry (vi)	lemaher	לְמַהֵר

15. The most important verbs. Part 3

to inform (vt)	leho'dia	לְהוֹדִיעַ
to insist (vi, vt)	lehit'akeʃ	לְהִתעַקֵש
to insult (vt)	leha'aliv	לְהַעֲלִיב
to invite (vt)	lehazmin	לְהַזמִין
to joke (vi)	lehitba'deax	לְהִתבַּדֵחַ

| to keep (vt) | liʃmor | לִשמוֹר |
| to keep silent, to hush | liʃtok | לִשתוֹק |

to kill (vt)	laharog	לַהֲרוֹג
to know (sb)	lehakir et	לְהַכִּיר אֶת
to know (sth)	la'da'at	לָדַעַת
to laugh (vi)	litsχok	לִצְחוֹק
to liberate (city, etc.)	leʃaχrer	לְשַׁחְרֵר
to look for ... (search)	leχapes	לְחַפֵּשׂ
to love (sb)	le'ehov	לֶאֱהוֹב
to make a mistake	lit'ot	לִטְעוֹת
to manage, to run	lenahel	לְנַהֵל
to mean (signify)	lomar	לוֹמַר
to mention (talk about)	lehazkir	לְהַזְכִּיר
to miss (school, etc.)	lehaχsir	לְהַחְסִיר
to notice (see)	lasim lev	לָשִׂים לֵב
to object (vi, vt)	lehitnaged	לְהִתְנַגֵּד
to observe (see)	litspot, lehaʃkif	לִצְפּוֹת, לְהַשְׁקִיף
to open (vt)	lif'toaχ	לִפְתּוֹחַ
to order (meal, etc.)	lehazmin	לְהַזְמִין
to order (mil.)	lifkod	לִפְקוֹד
to own (possess)	lihyot 'ba'al ʃel	לִהְיוֹת בַּעַל שֶׁל
to participate (vi)	lehiʃtatef	לְהִשְׁתַּתֵּף
to pay (vi, vt)	leʃalem	לְשַׁלֵּם
to permit (vt)	leharʃot	לְהַרְשׁוֹת
to plan (vt)	letaχnen	לְתַכְנֵן
to play (children)	lesaχek	לְשַׂחֵק
to pray (vi, vt)	lehitpalel	לְהִתְפַּלֵּל
to prefer (vt)	leha'adif	לְהַעֲדִיף
to promise (vt)	lehav'tiaχ	לְהַבְטִיחַ
to pronounce (vt)	levate	לְבַטֵּא
to propose (vt)	leha'tsi'a	לְהַצִּיעַ
to punish (vt)	leha'aniʃ	לְהַעֲנִישׁ

16. The most important verbs. Part 4

to read (vi, vt)	likro	לִקְרוֹא
to recommend (vt)	lehamlits	לְהַמְלִיץ
to refuse (vi, vt)	lesarev	לְסָרֵב
to regret (be sorry)	lehitsta'er	לְהִצְטַעֵר
to rent (sth from sb)	liskor	לִשְׂכּוֹר
to repeat (say again)	laχazor al	לַחֲזוֹר עַל
to reserve, to book	lehazmin meroʃ	לְהַזְמִין מֵרֹאשׁ
to run (vi)	laruts	לָרוּץ
to save (rescue)	lehatsil	לְהַצִּיל
to say (~ thank you)	lomar	לוֹמַר
to scold (vt)	linzof	לִנְזוֹף
to see (vt)	lir'ot	לִרְאוֹת
to sell (vt)	limkor	לִמְכּוֹר
to send (vt)	liʃ'loaχ	לִשְׁלוֹחַ

to shoot (vi)	lirot	לִירוֹת
to shout (vi)	liʦ'ok	לִצְעוֹק
to show (vt)	lehar'ot	לְהַרְאוֹת
to sign (document)	laxtom	לַחְתּוֹם
to sit down (vi)	lehityaʃev	לְהִתְיַשֵּׁב
to smile (vi)	lexayex	לְחַיֵּךְ
to speak (vi, vt)	ledaber	לְדַבֵּר
to steal (money, etc.)	lignov	לִגְנוֹב
to stop (for pause, etc.)	la'aʦor	לַעֲצוֹר
to stop (please ~ calling me)	lehafsik	לְהַפְסִיק
to study (vt)	lilmod	לִלְמוֹד
to swim (vi)	lisxot	לִשְׂחוֹת
to take (vt)	la'kaxat	לָקַחַת
to think (vi, vt)	laxʃov	לַחְשׁוֹב
to threaten (vt)	le'ayem	לְאַיֵּם
to touch (with hands)	la'ga'at	לָגַעַת
to translate (vt)	letargem	לְתַרְגֵּם
to trust (vt)	liv'toax	לִבְטוֹחַ
to try (attempt)	lenasot	לְנַסּוֹת
to turn (e.g., ~ left)	lifnot	לִפְנוֹת
to underestimate (vt)	leham'it be"erex	לְהַמְעִיט בְּעֶרְךְ
to understand (vt)	lehavin	לְהָבִין
to unite (vt)	le'axed	לְאַחֵד
to wait (vt)	lehamtin	לְהַמְתִּין
to want (wish, desire)	lirʦot	לִרְצוֹת
to warn (vt)	lehazhir	לְהַזְהִיר
to work (vi)	la'avod	לַעֲבוֹד
to write (vt)	lixtov	לִכְתּוֹב
to write down	lirʃom	לִרְשׁוֹם

TIME. CALENDAR

17. Weekdays

Monday	yom ʃeni	יוֹם שֵׁנִי (ז)
Tuesday	yom ʃliʃi	יוֹם שְׁלִישִׁי (ז)
Wednesday	yom revi'i	יוֹם רְבִיעִי (ז)
Thursday	yom xamiʃi	יוֹם חֲמִישִׁי (ז)
Friday	yom ʃiʃi	יוֹם שִׁישִׁי (ז)
Saturday	ʃabat	שַׁבָּת (נ)
Sunday	yom riʃon	יוֹם רִאשׁוֹן (ז)
today (adv)	hayom	הַיוֹם
tomorrow (adv)	maxar	מָחָר
the day after tomorrow	maxara'tayim	מָחֳרָתַיִם
yesterday (adv)	etmol	אֶתְמוֹל
the day before yesterday	ʃilʃom	שִׁלְשׁוֹם
day	yom	יוֹם (ז)
working day	yom avoda	יוֹם עֲבוֹדָה (ז)
public holiday	yom xag	יוֹם חַג (ז)
day off	yom menuxa	יוֹם מְנוּחָה (ז)
weekend	sof ʃa'vu'a	סוֹף שָׁבוּעַ
all day long	kol hayom	כָּל הַיוֹם
the next day (adv)	lamaxarat	לַמָחֳרָת
two days ago	lifnei yo'mayim	לִפְנֵי יוֹמַיִם
the day before	'erev	עֶרֶב
daily (adj)	yomyomi	יוֹמִיוֹמִי
every day (adv)	midei yom	מִדֵּי יוֹם
week	ʃa'vua	שָׁבוּעַ (ז)
last week (adv)	baʃa'vu'a ʃe'avar	בְּשָׁבוּעַ שֶׁעָבָר
next week (adv)	baʃa'vu'a haba	בְּשָׁבוּעַ הַבָּא
weekly (adj)	ʃvu'i	שְׁבוּעִי
every week (adv)	kol ʃa'vu'a	כָּל שָׁבוּעַ
twice a week	pa'a'mayim beʃa'vu'a	פַּעֲמַיִם בְּשָׁבוּעַ
every Tuesday	kol yom ʃliʃi	כָּל יוֹם שְׁלִישִׁי

18. Hours. Day and night

morning	'boker	בּוֹקֶר (ז)
in the morning	ba'boker	בַּבּוֹקֶר
noon, midday	tsaha'rayim	צָהֳרַיִם (ז"ר)
in the afternoon	axar hatsaha'rayim	אַחַר הַצָּהֳרַיִם
evening	'erev	עֶרֶב (ז)
in the evening	ba''erev	בָּעֶרֶב

night	'laila	לַיְלָה (ז)
at night	ba'laila	בַּלַּיְלָה
midnight	χatsot	חֲצוֹת (נ)
second	ʃniya	שְׁנִיָּה (נ)
minute	daka	דַּקָּה (נ)
hour	ʃa'a	שָׁעָה (נ)
half an hour	χatsi ʃa'a	חֲצִי שָׁעָה (נ)
a quarter-hour	'reva ʃa'a	רֶבַע שָׁעָה (ז)
fifteen minutes	χameʃ esre dakot	חֲמֵשׁ עָשְׂרֵה דַּקּוֹת
24 hours	yemama	יְמָמָה (נ)
sunrise	zriχa	זְרִיחָה (נ)
dawn	'ʃaχar	שַׁחַר (ז)
early morning	'ʃaχar	שַׁחַר (ז)
sunset	ʃki'a	שְׁקִיעָה (נ)
early in the morning	mukdam ba'boker	מוּקְדָּם בַּבּוֹקֶר
this morning	ha'boker	הַבּוֹקֶר
tomorrow morning	maχar ba'boker	מָחָר בַּבּוֹקֶר
this afternoon	hayom aχarei hatzaha'rayim	הַיּוֹם אַחֲרֵי הַצָּהֳרַיִים
in the afternoon	aχar hatsaha'rayim	אַחַר הַצָּהֳרַיִים
tomorrow afternoon	maχar aχarei hatsaha'rayim	מָחָר אַחֲרֵי הַצָּהֳרַיִים
tonight (this evening)	ha''erev	הָעֶרֶב
tomorrow night	maχar ba''erev	מָחָר בָּעֶרֶב
at 3 o'clock sharp	baʃa'a ʃaloʃ bediyuk	בְּשָׁעָה שָׁלוֹשׁ בְּדִיּוּק
about 4 o'clock	bisvivot arba	בִּסְבִיבוֹת אַרְבַּע
by 12 o'clock	ad ʃteim esre	עַד שְׁתַּיִם-עָשְׂרֵה
in 20 minutes	be'od esrim dakot	בְּעוֹד עֶשְׂרִים דַּקּוֹת
in an hour	be'od ʃa'a	בְּעוֹד שָׁעָה
on time (adv)	bazman	בַּזְּמַן
a quarter to …	'reva le…	רֶבַע לְ...
within an hour	toχ ʃa'a	תּוֹךְ שָׁעָה
every 15 minutes	kol 'reva ʃa'a	כָּל רֶבַע שָׁעָה
round the clock	misaviv laʃa'on	מִסָּבִיב לַשָּׁעוֹן

19. Months. Seasons

January	'yanu'ar	יָנוּאָר (ז)
February	'febru'ar	פֶבְּרוּאָר (ז)
March	merts	מֶרְץ (ז)
April	april	אַפְּרִיל (ז)
May	mai	מַאי (ז)
June	'yuni	יוּנִי (ז)
July	'yuli	יוּלִי (ז)
August	'ogust	אוֹגוּסְט (ז)
September	sep'tember	סֶפְּטֶמְבָּר (ז)
October	ok'tober	אוֹקְטוֹבָּר (ז)

November	no'vember	נוֹבֶמבָּר (ז)
December	de'tsember	דֶצֶמבָּר (ז)
spring	aviv	אָבִיב (ז)
in spring	ba'aviv	בָּאָבִיב
spring (as adj)	avivi	אָבִיבִי
summer	'kayits	קַיִץ (ז)
in summer	ba'kayits	בַּקַיִץ
summer (as adj)	ketsi	קֵיצִי
autumn	stav	סתָיו (ז)
in autumn	bestav	בַּסתָיו
autumn (as adj)	stavi	סתָווִי
winter	'χoref	חוֹרֶף (ז)
in winter	ba'χoref	בַּחוֹרֶף
winter (as adj)	χorpi	חוֹרפִּי
month	'χodeʃ	חוֹדֶשׁ (ז)
this month	ha'χodeʃ	הַחוֹדֶשׁ
next month	ba'χodeʃ haba	בַּחוֹדֶשׁ הַבָּא
last month	ba'χodeʃ ʃe'avar	בַּחוֹדֶשׁ שֶׁעָבַר
a month ago	lifnei 'χodeʃ	לִפנֵי חוֹדֶשׁ
in a month (a month later)	be'od 'χodeʃ	בְּעוֹד חוֹדֶשׁ
in 2 months (2 months later)	be'od χod'ʃayim	בְּעוֹד חוֹדשַׁיִים
the whole month	kol ha'χodeʃ	כָּל הַחוֹדֶשׁ
all month long	kol ha'χodeʃ	כָּל הַחוֹדֶשׁ
monthly (~ magazine)	χodʃi	חוֹדשִׁי
monthly (adv)	χodʃit	חוֹדשִׁית
every month	kol 'χodeʃ	כָּל חוֹדֶשׁ
twice a month	pa'a'mayim be'χodeʃ	פַּעֲמַיִים בְּחוֹדֶשׁ
year	ʃana	שָׁנָה (נ)
this year	haʃana	הַשָׁנָה
next year	baʃana haba'a	בָּשָׁנָה הַבָּאָה
last year	baʃana ʃe'avra	בָּשָׁנָה שֶׁעָברָה
a year ago	lifnei ʃana	לִפנֵי שָׁנָה
in a year	be'od ʃana	בְּעוֹד שָׁנָה
in two years	be'od ʃna'tayim	בְּעוֹד שְׁנָתַיִים
the whole year	kol haʃana	כָּל הַשָׁנָה
all year long	kol haʃana	כָּל הַשָׁנָה
every year	kol ʃana	כָּל שָׁנָה
annual (adj)	ʃnati	שְׁנָתִי
annually (adv)	midei ʃana	מִדֵי שָׁנָה
4 times a year	arba pa'amim be'χodeʃ	אַרבַּע פְּעָמִים בְּחוֹדֶשׁ
date (e.g. today's ~)	ta'ariχ	תַאָרִיך (ז)
date (e.g. ~ of birth)	ta'ariχ	תַאָרִיך (ז)
calendar	'luaχ ʃana	לוּחַ שָׁנָה (ז)
half a year	χatsi ʃana	חֲצִי שָׁנָה (ז)
six months	ʃiʃa χodaʃim, χatsi ʃana	חֲצִי שָׁנָה, שִׁישָׁה חוֹדָשִׁים

| season (summer, etc.) | ona | עוֹנָה (נ) |
| century | 'me'a | מֵאָה (נ) |

TRAVEL. HOTEL

20. Trip. Travel

tourism, travel	tayarut	תַּיָּירוּת (נ)
tourist	tayar	תַּיָּיר (ז)
trip, voyage	tiyul	טִיּוּל (ז)
adventure	harpatka	הַרְפַּתְקָה (נ)
trip, journey	nesi'a	נְסִיעָה (נ)
holiday	χufʃa	חוּפְשָׁה (נ)
to be on holiday	lihyot beχufʃa	לִהְיוֹת בְּחוּפְשָׁה
rest	menuχa	מְנוּחָה (נ)
train	ra'kevet	רַכֶּבֶת (נ)
by train	bera'kevet	בְּרַכֶּבֶת
aeroplane	matos	מָטוֹס (ז)
by aeroplane	bematos	בְּמָטוֹס
by car	bemeχonit	בִּמְכוֹנִית
by ship	be'oniya	בְּאוֹנִיָּיה
luggage	mit'an	מִטְעָן (ז)
suitcase	mizvada	מִזְוָודָה (נ)
luggage trolley	eglat mit'an	עֶגְלַת מִטְעָן (נ)
passport	darkon	דַּרְכּוֹן (ז)
visa	'viza, aʃra	וִיזָה, אַשְׁרָה (נ)
ticket	kartis	כַּרְטִיס (ז)
air ticket	kartis tisa	כַּרְטִיס טִיסָה (ז)
guidebook	madriχ	מַדְרִיךְ (ז)
map (tourist ~)	mapa	מַפָּה (נ)
area (rural ~)	ezor	אֵזוֹר (ז)
place, site	makom	מָקוֹם (ז)
exotica (n)	ek'zotika	אֶקְזוֹטִיקָה (נ)
exotic (adj)	ek'zoti	אֶקְזוֹטִי
amazing (adj)	nifla	נִפְלָא
group	kvutsa	קְבוּצָה (נ)
excursion, sightseeing tour	tiyul	טִיּוּל (ז)
guide (person)	madriχ tiyulim	מַדְרִיךְ טִיּוּלִים (ז)

21. Hotel

hotel	malon	מָלוֹן (ז)
motel	motel	מוֹטֶל (ז)
three-star (~ hotel)	ʃloʃa koχavim	שְׁלוֹשָׁה כּוֹכָבִים

five-star	χamiʃa koχavim	חֲמִישָׁה כּוֹכָבִים
to stay (in a hotel, etc.)	lehit'aχsen	לְהִתְאַכְסֵן
room	'χeder	חֶדֶר (ז)
single room	'χeder yaχid	חֶדֶר יָחִיד (ז)
double room	'χeder zugi	חֶדֶר זוּגִי (ז)
to book a room	lehazmin 'χeder	לְהַזְמִין חֶדֶר
half board	χatsi pensiyon	חֲצִי פֶּנְסְיוֹן (ז)
full board	pensyon male	פֶּנְסְיוֹן מָלֵא (ז)
with bath	im am'batya	עִם אַמְבַּטְיָה
with shower	im mik'laχat	עִם מִקְלַחַת
satellite television	tele'vizya bekvalim	טֶלֶוִיזְיָה בְּכְבָלִים (נ)
air-conditioner	mazgan	מַזְגָן (ז)
towel	ma'gevet	מַגֶּבֶת (נ)
key	maf'teaχ	מַפְתֵּחַ (ז)
administrator	amarkal	אֲמַרְכָּל (ז)
chambermaid	χadranit	חַדְרָנִית (נ)
porter	sabal	סַבָּל (ז)
doorman	pakid kabala	פְּקִיד קַבָּלָה (ז)
restaurant	mis'ada	מִסְעָדָה (נ)
pub, bar	bar	בָּר (ז)
breakfast	aruχat 'boker	אֲרוּחַת בּוֹקֶר (נ)
dinner	aruχat 'erev	אֲרוּחַת עֶרֶב (נ)
buffet	miznon	מִזְנוֹן (ז)
lobby	'lobi	לוֹבִּי (ז)
lift	ma'alit	מַעֲלִית (נ)
DO NOT DISTURB	lo lehaf'ri'a	לֹא לְהַפְרִיעַ
NO SMOKING	asur le'aʃen!	אָסוּר לְעַשֵׁן!

22. Sightseeing

monument	an'darta	אַנְדַּרְטָה (נ)
fortress	mivtsar	מִבְצָר (ז)
palace	armon	אַרְמוֹן (ז)
castle	tira	טִירָה (נ)
tower	migdal	מִגְדָל (ז)
mausoleum	ma'uzo'le'um	מָאוֹזוֹלֵיאוּם (ז)
architecture	adriχalut	אַדְרִיכָלוּת (נ)
medieval (adj)	benaimi	בֵּינַיימִי
ancient (adj)	atik	עַתִּיק
national (adj)	le'umi	לְאוּמִי
famous (monument, etc.)	mefursam	מְפוּרְסָם
tourist	tayar	תַּיָיר (ז)
guide (person)	madriχ tiyulim	מַדְרִיךְ טִיוּלִים (ז)
excursion, sightseeing tour	tiyul	טִיוּל (ז)
to show (vt)	lehar'ot	לְהַרְאוֹת

to tell (vt)	lesaper	לְסַפֵּר
to find (vt)	limtso	לִמְצוֹא
to get lost (lose one's way)	la'leχet le'ibud	לָלֶכֶת לְאִיבּוּד
map (e.g. underground ~)	mapa	מַפָּה (נ)
map (e.g. city ~)	tarʃim	תַּרְשִׁים (ז)
souvenir, gift	maz'keret	מַזְכֶּרֶת (נ)
gift shop	χanut matanot	חֲנוּת מַתָּנוֹת (נ)
to take pictures	letsalem	לְצַלֵם
to have one's picture taken	lehitstalem	לְהִצְטַלֵם

TRANSPORT

23. Airport

airport	nemal teʕufa	נְמַל תְּעוּפָה (ז)
aeroplane	matos	מָטוֹס (ז)
airline	xevrat teʕufa	חֶבְרַת תְּעוּפָה (נ)
air traffic controller	bakar tisa	בַּקָר טִיסָה (ז)
departure	hamraʼa	הַמְרָאָה (נ)
arrival	nexita	נְחִיתָה (נ)
to arrive (by plane)	lehaʼgiʼa betisa	לְהַגִּיעַ בְּטִיסָה
departure time	zman hamraʼa	זְמַן הַמְרָאָה (ז)
arrival time	zman nexita	זְמַן נְחִיתָה (ז)
to be delayed	lehitʕakev	לְהִתְעַכֵּב
flight delay	ikuv hatisa	עִכּוּב הַטִּיסָה (ז)
information board	ʼluax meida	לוּחַ מֵידָע (ז)
information	meida	מֵידָע (ז)
to announce (vt)	lehoʼdia	לְהוֹדִיעַ
flight (e.g. next ~)	tisa	טִיסָה (נ)
customs	ʼmexes	מֶכֶס (ז)
customs officer	pakid ʼmexes	פָּקִיד מֶכֶס (ז)
customs declaration	hatsharat mexes	הַצְהָרַת מֶכֶס (נ)
to fill in (vt)	lemale	לְמַלֵּא
to fill in the declaration	lemale ʼtofes hatshara	לְמַלֵּא טוֹפֶס הַצְהָרָה
passport control	bdikat darkonim	בְּדִיקַת דַּרְכּוֹנִים (נ)
luggage	kvuda	כְּבוּדָה (נ)
hand luggage	kvudat yad	כְּבוּדַת יָד (נ)
luggage trolley	eglat kvuda	עֶגְלַת כְּבוּדָה (נ)
landing	nexita	נְחִיתָה (נ)
landing strip	maslul nexita	מַסְלוּל נְחִיתָה (ז)
to land (vi)	linxot	לִנְחוֹת
airstair (passenger stair)	ʼkeveʃ	כֶּבֶשׁ (ז)
check-in	tʃek in	צֶ׳ק אִין (ז)
check-in counter	dalpak tʃek in	דַּלְפַּק צֶ׳ק אִין (ז)
to check-in (vi)	levaʼtseʼa tʃek in	לְבַצֵּעַ צֶ׳ק אִין
boarding card	kartis aliya lematos	כַּרְטִיס עֲלִיָּה לְמָטוֹס (ז)
departure gate	ʼʃaʕar yetsiʼa	שַׁעַר יְצִיאָה (ז)
transit	maʕavar	מַעֲבָר (ז)
to wait (vt)	lehamtin	לְהַמְתִּין
departure lounge	traklin tisa	טְרַקְלִין טִיסָה (ז)

| to see off | lelavot | לְלַוּוֹת |
| to say goodbye | lomar lehitra'ot | לוֹמַר לְהִתְרָאוֹת |

24. Aeroplane

aeroplane	matos	מָטוֹס (ז)
air ticket	kartis tisa	כַּרְטִיס טִיסָה (ז)
airline	χevrat te'ufa	חֶבְרַת תְּעוּפָה (נ)
airport	nemal te'ufa	נְמַל תְּעוּפָה (ז)
supersonic (adj)	al koli	עַל קוֹלִי

captain	kabarnit	קַבַּרְנִיט (ז)
crew	'tsevet	צֶוֶת (ז)
pilot	tayas	טַיָּס (ז)
stewardess	da'yelet	דַּיֶּלֶת (נ)
navigator	navat	נַוָּט (ז)

wings	kna'fayim	כְּנָפַיִם (נ"ר)
tail	zanav	זָנָב (ז)
cockpit	'kokpit	קוֹקְפִּיט (ז)
engine	ma'no'a	מָנוֹעַ (ז)
undercarriage (landing gear)	kan nesi'a	כַּן נְסִיעָה (ז)
turbine	tur'bina	טוּרְבִּינָה (נ)
propeller	madχef	מַדְחֵף (ז)
black box	kufsa ʃχora	קוּפְסָה שְׁחוֹרָה (נ)
yoke (control column)	'hege	הֶגֶה (ז)
fuel	'delek	דֶּלֶק (ז)

safety card	hora'ot betiχut	הוֹרָאוֹת בְּטִיחוּת (נ"ר)
oxygen mask	maseχat χamtsan	מַסֵּיכַת חַמְצָן (נ)
uniform	madim	מַדִּים (ז"ר)
lifejacket	χagorat hatsala	חֲגוֹרַת הַצָּלָה (נ)
parachute	mitsnaχ	מִצְנָח (ז)
takeoff	hamra'a	הַמְרָאָה (נ)
to take off (vi)	lehamri	לְהַמְרִיא
runway	maslul hamra'a	מַסְלוּל הַמְרָאָה (ז)

visibility	re'ut	רְאוּת (נ)
flight (act of flying)	tisa	טִיסָה (נ)
altitude	'gova	גּוֹבַהּ (ז)
air pocket	kis avir	כִּיס אֲוִויר (ז)

seat	moʃav	מוֹשָׁב (ז)
headphones	ozniyot	אוֹזְנִיּוֹת (נ"ר)
folding tray (tray table)	magaʃ mitkapel	מַגָּשׁ מִתְקַפֵּל (ז)
airplane window	tsohar	צוֹהַר (ז)
aisle	ma'avar	מַעֲבָר (ז)

25. Train

| train | ra'kevet | רַכֶּבֶת (נ) |
| commuter train | ra'kevet parvarim | רַכֶּבֶת פַּרְבָרִים (נ) |

express train	ra'kevet mehira	רַכֶּבֶת מְהִירָה (נ)
diesel locomotive	katar 'dizel	קַטָּר דִּיזֶל (ז)
steam locomotive	katar	קַטָּר (ז)
coach, carriage	karon	קָרוֹן (ז)
buffet car	kron mis'ada	קְרוֹן מִסְעָדָה (ז)
rails	mesilot	מְסִילּוֹת (נ"ר)
railway	mesilat barzel	מְסִילַת בַּרְזֶל (נ)
sleeper (track support)	'eden	אֶדֶן (ז)
platform (railway ~)	ratsif	רָצִיף (ז)
platform (~ 1, 2, etc.)	mesila	מְסִילָה (נ)
semaphore	ramzor	רַמְזוֹר (ז)
station	taxana	תַּחֲנָה (נ)
train driver	nahag ra'kevet	נַהָג רַכֶּבֶת (ז)
porter (of luggage)	sabal	סַבָּל (ז)
carriage attendant	sadran ra'kevet	סַדְרָן רַכֶּבֶת (ז)
passenger	no'se'a	נוֹסֵעַ (ז)
ticket inspector	bodek	בּוֹדֵק (ז)
corridor (in train)	prozdor	פְּרוֹזְדוֹר (ז)
emergency brake	ma'atsar xirum	מַעֲצַר חֵירוּם (ז)
compartment	ta	תָּא (ז)
berth	dargaʃ	דַּרְגָּשׁ (ז)
upper berth	dargaʃ elyon	דַּרְגָּשׁ עֶלְיוֹן (ז)
lower berth	dargaʃ taxton	דַּרְגָּשׁ תַּחְתּוֹן (ז)
bed linen, bedding	matsa'im	מַצָּעִים (ז"ר)
ticket	kartis	כַּרְטִיס (ז)
timetable	'luax zmanim	לוּחַ זְמַנִּים (ז)
information display	'ʃelet meida	שֶׁלֶט מֵידָע (ז)
to leave, to depart	latset	לָצֵאת
departure (of a train)	yetsi'a	יְצִיאָה (נ)
to arrive (ab. train)	leha'gi'a	לְהַגִּיעַ
arrival	haga'a	הַגָּעָה (נ)
to arrive by train	leha'gi'a bera'kevet	לְהַגִּיעַ בְּרַכֶּבֶת
to get on the train	la'alot lera'kevet	לַעֲלוֹת לְרַכֶּבֶת
to get off the train	la'redet mehara'kevet	לָרֶדֶת מֵהָרַכֶּבֶת
train crash	hitraskut	הִתְרַסְּקוּת (נ)
to derail (vi)	la'redet mipasei ra'kevet	לָרֶדֶת מִפַּסֵּי רַכֶּבֶת
steam locomotive	katar	קַטָּר (ז)
stoker, fireman	masik	מַסִּיק (ז)
firebox	kivʃan	כִּבְשָׁן (ז)
coal	pexam	פֶּחָם (ז)

26. Ship

ship	sfina	סְפִינָה (נ)
vessel	sfina	סְפִינָה (נ)

steamship	oniyat kitor	אוֹנִיַּת קִיטוֹר (נ)
riverboat	sfinat nahar	סְפִינַת נָהָר (נ)
cruise ship	oniyat ta'anugot	אוֹנִיַּת תַּעֲנוּגוֹת (נ)
cruiser	sa'yeret	סַיֶּרֶת (נ)
yacht	'yaχta	יַכְטָה (נ)
tugboat	go'reret	גוֹרֶרֶת (נ)
barge	arba	אַרְבָּה (נ)
ferry	ma'a'boret	מַעֲבּוֹרֶת (נ)
sailing ship	sfinat mifras	סְפִינַת מִפְרָשׂ (נ)
brigantine	briganit	בְּרִיגָנִית (נ)
ice breaker	ʃo'veret 'keraχ	שׁוֹבֶרֶת קֶרַח (נ)
submarine	tso'lelet	צוֹלֶלֶת (נ)
boat (flat-bottomed ~)	sira	סִירָה (נ)
dinghy (lifeboat)	sira	סִירָה (נ)
lifeboat	sirat hatsala	סִירַת הַצָּלָה (נ)
motorboat	sirat ma'no'a	סִירַת מָנוֹע (נ)
captain	rav χovel	רַב־חוֹבֵל (ז)
seaman	malaχ	מַלָּח (ז)
sailor	yamai	יַמַּאי (ז)
crew	'tsevet	צֶוֶת (ז)
boatswain	rav malaχim	רַב־מַלָּחִים (ז)
ship's boy	'na'ar sipun	נַעַר סִיפּוּן (ז)
cook	tabaχ	טַבָּח (ז)
ship's doctor	rofe ha'oniya	רוֹפֵא הָאוֹנִיָּיה (ז)
deck	sipun	סִיפּוּן (ז)
mast	'toren	תּוֹרֶן (ז)
sail	mifras	מִפְרָשׂ (ז)
hold	'beten oniya	בֶּטֶן אוֹנִיָּיה (נ)
bow (prow)	χartom	חַרְטוֹם (ז)
stern	yarketei hasfina	יַרְכְּתֵי הַסְּפִינָה (ז"ר)
oar	maʃot	מָשׁוֹט (ז)
screw propeller	madχef	מַדְחֵף (ז)
cabin	ta	תָּא (ז)
wardroom	mo'adon ktsinim	מוֹעֲדוֹן קְצִינִים (ז)
engine room	χadar meχonot	חֲדַר מְכוֹנוֹת (ז)
bridge	'geʃer hapikud	גֶּשֶׁר הַפִּיקוּד (ז)
radio room	ta alχutan	תָּא אַלְחוּטָן (ז)
wave (radio)	'teder	תֶּדֶר (ז)
logbook	yoman ha'oniya	יוֹמָן הָאוֹנִיָּיה (ז)
spyglass	miʃkefet	מִשְׁקֶפֶת (נ)
bell	pa'amon	פַּעֲמוֹן (ז)
flag	'degel	דֶּגֶל (ז)
hawser (mooring ~)	avot ha'oniya	עֲבוֹת הָאוֹנִיָּיה (נ)
knot (bowline, etc.)	'keʃer	קֶשֶׁר (ז)
deckrails	ma'ake hasipun	מַעֲקֵה הַסִּיפּוּן (ז)

gangway	'keveʃ	כֶּבֶשׁ (ז)
anchor	'ogen	עוֹגֶן (ז)
to weigh anchor	leharim 'ogen	לְהָרִים עוֹגֶן
to drop anchor	la'agon	לַעֲגוֹן
anchor chain	ʃar'ʃeret ha'ogen	שַׁרְשֶׁרֶת הָעוֹגֶן (נ)
port (harbour)	namal	נָמֵל (ז)
quay, wharf	'mezax	מֶזַח (ז)
to berth (moor)	la'agon	לַעֲגוֹן
to cast off	lehaflig	לְהַפְלִיג
trip, voyage	masa, tiyul	מַסָּע (ז), טִיּוּל (ז)
cruise (sea trip)	'ʃayit	שַׁיִט (ז)
course (route)	kivun	כִּיווּן (ז)
route (itinerary)	nativ	נָתִיב (ז)
fairway (safe water channel)	nativ 'ʃayit	נָתִיב שַׁיִט (ז)
shallows	sirton	שִׂרְטוֹן (ז)
to run aground	la'alot al hasirton	לַעֲלוֹת עַל הַשִּׂרְטוֹן
storm	sufa	סוּפָה (נ)
signal	ot	אוֹת (ז)
to sink (vi)	lit'bo'a	לִטְבּוֹעַ
Man overboard!	adam ba'mayim!	אָדָם בַּמַּיִם!
SOS (distress signal)	kri'at hatsala	קְרִיאַת הַצָּלָה
ring buoy	galgal hatsala	גַּלְגַּל הַצָּלָה (ז)

CITY

27. Urban transport

bus, coach	'otobus	אוֹטוֹבּוּס (ז)
tram	ra'kevet kala	רַכֶּבֶת קַלָּה (נ)
trolleybus	tro'leibus	טְרוֹלֵיבּוּס (ז)
route (bus ~)	maslul	מַסְלוּל (ז)
number (e.g. bus ~)	mispar	מִסְפָּר (ז)
to go by …	lin'so'a be…	לִנְסוֹעַ בְּ...
to get on (~ the bus)	la'alot	לַעֲלוֹת
to get off …	la'redet mi…	לָרֶדֶת מִ...
stop (e.g. bus ~)	taχana	תַּחֲנָה (נ)
next stop	hataχana haba'a	הַתַּחֲנָה הַבָּאָה (נ)
terminus	hataχana ha'aχrona	הַתַּחֲנָה הָאַחֲרוֹנָה (נ)
timetable	'luaχ zmanim	לוּחַ זְמַנִּים (ז)
to wait (vt)	lehamtin	לְהַמְתִּין
ticket	kartis	כַּרְטִיס (ז)
fare	meχir hanesiya	מְחִיר הַנְּסִיעָה (ז)
cashier (ticket seller)	kupai	קוּפַּאי (ז)
ticket inspection	bi'koret kartisim	בִּיקּוֹרֶת כַּרְטִיסִים (נ)
ticket inspector	mevaker	מְבַקֵּר (ז)
to be late (for …)	le'aχer	לְאַחֵר
to miss (~ the train, etc.)	lefasfes	לְפַסְפֵּס
to be in a hurry	lemaher	לְמַהֵר
taxi, cab	monit	מוֹנִית (נ)
taxi driver	nahag monit	נַהַג מוֹנִית (ז)
by taxi	bemonit	בְּמוֹנִית
taxi rank	taχanat moniyot	תַּחֲנַת מוֹנִיּוֹת (נ)
to call a taxi	lehazmin monit	לְהַזְמִין מוֹנִית
to take a taxi	la'kaχat monit	לָקַחַת מוֹנִית
traffic	tnu'a	תְּנוּעָה (נ)
traffic jam	pkak	פְּקָק (ז)
rush hour	ʃa'ot 'omes	שְׁעוֹת עוֹמֶס (נ"ר)
to park (vi)	laχanot	לַחֲנוֹת
to park (vt)	lehaχnot	לְהַחֲנוֹת
car park	χanaya	חֲנָיָה (נ)
underground, tube	ra'kevet taχtit	רַכֶּבֶת תַּחְתִּית (נ)
station	taχana	תַּחֲנָה (נ)
to take the tube	lin'so'a betaχtit	לִנְסוֹעַ בְּתַחְתִּית
train	ra'kevet	רַכֶּבֶת (נ)
train station	taχanat ra'kevet	תַּחֲנַת רַכֶּבֶת (נ)

28. City. Life in the city

city, town	ir	עִיר (נ)
capital city	ir bira	עִיר בִּירָה (נ)
village	kfar	כְּפָר (ז)
city map	mapat ha'ir	מַפַּת הָעִיר (נ)
city centre	merkaz ha'ir	מֶרְכַּז הָעִיר (ז)
suburb	parvar	פַּרְוָר (ז)
suburban (adj)	parvari	פַּרְוָרִי
outskirts	parvar	פַּרְוָר (ז)
environs (suburbs)	svivot	סְבִיבוֹת (נ"ר)
city block	ʃxuna	שְׁכוּנָה (נ)
residential block (area)	ʃxunat megurim	שְׁכוּנַת מְגוּרִים (נ)
traffic	tnu'a	תְּנוּעָה (נ)
traffic lights	ramzor	רַמְזוֹר (ז)
public transport	taxbura tsiburit	תַּחְבּוּרָה צִיבּוּרִית (נ)
crossroads	'tsomet	צוֹמֶת (ז)
zebra crossing	ma'avar xatsaya	מַעֲבָר חֲצָיָה (ז)
pedestrian subway	ma'avar tat karka'i	מַעֲבָר תַּת-קַרְקָעִי (ז)
to cross (~ the street)	laxatsot	לַחֲצוֹת
pedestrian	holex 'regel	הוֹלֵךְ רֶגֶל (ז)
pavement	midraxa	מִדְרָכָה (נ)
bridge	'geʃer	גֶּשֶׁר (ז)
embankment (river walk)	ta'yelet	טַיֶּלֶת (נ)
fountain	mizraka	מִזְרָקָה (נ)
allée (garden walkway)	sdera	שְׂדֵרָה (נ)
park	park	פַּארְק (ז)
boulevard	sdera	שְׂדֵרָה (נ)
square	kikar	כִּיכָּר (נ)
avenue (wide street)	rexov raʃi	רְחוֹב רָאשִׁי (ז)
street	rexov	רְחוֹב (ז)
side street	simta	סִמְטָה (נ)
dead end	mavoi satum	מָבוֹי סָתוּם (ז)
house	'bayit	בַּיִת (ז)
building	binyan	בִּנְיָן (ז)
skyscraper	gored ʃxakim	גּוֹרֵד שְׁחָקִים (ז)
facade	xazit	חָזִית (נ)
roof	gag	גַּג (ז)
window	xalon	חַלּוֹן (ז)
arch	'keʃet	קֶשֶׁת (נ)
column	amud	עַמּוּד (ז)
corner	pina	פִּינָה (נ)
shop window	xalon ra'ava	חַלּוֹן רַאֲוָה (ז)
signboard (store sign, etc.)	'ʃelet	שֶׁלֶט (ז)
poster (e.g., playbill)	kraza	כְּרָזָה (נ)
advertising poster	'poster	פּוֹסְטֶר (ז)

hoarding	'luaχ pirsum	לוּחַ פִּרסוּם (ז)
rubbish	'zevel	זֶבֶל (ז)
rubbish bin	paχ aʃpa	פַּח אַשפָּה (ז)
to litter (vi)	lelaχleχ	לְלַכלֵך
rubbish dump	mizbala	מִזבָּלָה (נ)
telephone box	ta 'telefon	תָא טֶלֶפוֹן (ז)
lamppost	amud panas	עַמוּד פָּנָס (ז)
bench (park ~)	safsal	סַפסָל (ז)
police officer	ʃoter	שוֹטֵר (ז)
police	miʃtara	מִשטָרָה (נ)
beggar	kabtsan	קַבּצָן (ז)
homeless (n)	χasar 'bayit	חֲסַר בַּיִת (ז)

29. Urban institutions

shop	χanut	חֲנוּת (נ)
chemist, pharmacy	beit mir'kaχat	בֵּית מִרקַחַת (ז)
optician (spectacles shop)	χanut miʃka'fayim	חֲנוּת מִשקָפַיִים (נ)
shopping centre	kanyon	קַניוֹן (ז)
supermarket	super'market	סוּפֶּרמַרקֶט (ז)
bakery	ma'afiya	מַאֲפִייָה (נ)
baker	ofe	אוֹפֶה (ז)
cake shop	χanut mamtakim	חֲנוּת מַמתַקִים (נ)
grocery shop	ma'kolet	מַכּוֹלֶת (נ)
butcher shop	itliz	אִטלִיז (ז)
greengrocer	χanut perot viyerakot	חֲנוּת פֵּירוֹת וְיֶרָקוֹת (נ)
market	ʃuk	שוּק (ז)
coffee bar	beit kafe	בֵּית קָפֶה (ז)
restaurant	mis'ada	מִסעָדָה (נ)
pub, bar	pab	פָּאבּ (ז)
pizzeria	pi'tseriya	פִּיצֶרִייָה (נ)
hairdresser	mispara	מִספָּרָה (נ)
post office	'do'ar	דוֹאַר (ז)
dry cleaners	nikui yaveʃ	נִיקוּי יָבֵש (ז)
photo studio	'studyo letsilum	סטוּדִיוֹ לְצִילוּם (ז)
shoe shop	χanut na'a'layim	חֲנוּת נַעֲלַיִים (נ)
bookshop	χanut sfarim	חֲנוּת סְפָרִים (נ)
sports shop	χanut sport	חֲנוּת ספּוֹרט (נ)
clothes repair shop	χanut tikun bgadim	חֲנוּת תִיקוּן בּגָדִים (נ)
formal wear hire	χanut haskarat bgadim	חֲנוּת הַשֹֹכָּרַת בּגָדִים (נ)
video rental shop	χanut haʃʔalat sratim	חֲנוּת הַשאָלַת סְרָטִים (נ)
circus	kirkas	קִרקָס (ז)
zoo	gan hayot	גַן חַיוֹת (ז)
cinema	kol'no'a	קוֹלנוֹעַ (ז)
museum	muze'on	מוּזֵיאוֹן (ז)

library	sifriya	סִפְרִיָּה (נ)
theatre	te'atron	תֵּיאַטרוֹן (ז)
opera (opera house)	beit 'opera	בֵּית אוֹפֶּרָה (ז)
nightclub	mo'adon 'laila	מוֹעֲדוֹן לַילָה (ז)
casino	ka'zino	קָזִינוֹ (ז)
mosque	misgad	מִסגָּד (ז)
synagogue	beit 'kneset	בֵּית כְּנֶסֶת (ז)
cathedral	kated'rala	קָתֶדרָלָה (נ)
temple	mikdaʃ	מִקדָשׁ (ז)
church	knesiya	כְּנֵסִיָּה (נ)
college	miχlala	מִכלָלָה (נ)
university	uni'versita	אוּנִיבֶרסִיטָה (נ)
school	beit 'sefer	בֵּית סֵפֶר (ז)
prefecture	maχoz	מָחוֹז (ז)
town hall	iriya	עִירִיָּה (נ)
hotel	beit malon	בֵּית מָלוֹן (ז)
bank	bank	בַּנק (ז)
embassy	ʃagrirut	שַׁגרִירוּת (נ)
travel agency	soχnut nesi'ot	סוֹכנוּת נְסִיעוֹת (נ)
information office	modi'in	מוֹדִיעִין (ז)
currency exchange	misrad hamarat mat'be'a	מִשׂרַד הֲמָרַת מַטבֵּעַ (ז)
underground, tube	ra'kevet taχtit	רַכֶּבֶת תַּחתִּית (נ)
hospital	beit χolim	בֵּית חוֹלִים (ז)
petrol station	taχanat 'delek	תַּחֲנַת דֶלֶק (נ)
car park	migraʃ χanaya	מִגרַשׁ חֲנָיָה (ז)

30. Signs

signboard (store sign, etc.)	'ʃelet	שֶׁלֶט (ז)
notice (door sign, etc.)	moda'a	מוֹדָעָה (נ)
poster	'poster	פּוֹסטֶר (ז)
direction sign	tamrur	תַּמרוּר (ז)
arrow (sign)	χets	חֵץ (ז)
caution	azhara	אַזהָרָה (נ)
warning sign	'ʃelet azhara	שֶׁלֶט אַזהָרָה (ז)
to warn (vt)	lehazhir	לְהַזהִיר
rest day (weekly ~)	yom 'χofeʃ	יוֹם חוֹפֶשׁ (ז)
timetable (schedule)	'luaχ zmanim	לוּחַ זְמַנִים (ז)
opening hours	ʃa'ot avoda	שְׁעוֹת עֲבוֹדָה (נ"ר)
WELCOME!	bruχim haba'im!	ברוּכִים הַבָּאִים!
ENTRANCE	knisa	כְּנִיסָה
WAY OUT	yetsi'a	יְצִיאָה
PUSH	dχof	דחוֹף
PULL	mʃoχ	משׁוֹך

| OPEN | pa'tuax | פָּתוּחַ |
| CLOSED | sagur | סָגוּר |

| WOMEN | lenaʃim | לְנָשִׁים |
| MEN | legvarim | לִגְבָרִים |

DISCOUNTS	hanaxot	הֲנָחוֹת
SALE	mivtsa	מִבְצָע
NEW!	xadaʃ!	חָדָשׁ!
FREE	xinam	חִינָם

ATTENTION!	sim lev!	שִׂים לֵב!
NO VACANCIES	ein makom panui	אֵין מָקוֹם פָּנוּי
RESERVED	ʃamur	שָׁמוּר

| ADMINISTRATION | hanhala | הַנְהָלָה |
| STAFF ONLY | le'ovdim bilvad | לְעוֹבְדִים בִּלְבָד |

BEWARE OF THE DOG!	zehirut 'kelev noʃex!	זְהִירוּת, כֶּלֶב נוֹשֵׁךְ!
NO SMOKING	asur le'aʃen!	אָסוּר לְעַשֵׁן!
DO NOT TOUCH!	lo lagaat!	לֹא לָגַעַת!

DANGEROUS	mesukan	מְסוּכָּן
DANGER	sakana	סַכָּנָה
HIGH VOLTAGE	'metax ga'voha	מֶתַח גָּבוֹהַ
NO SWIMMING!	haraxatsa asura!	הָרַחֲצָה אֲסוּרָה!
OUT OF ORDER	lo oved	לֹא עוֹבֵד

FLAMMABLE	dalik	דָּלִיק
FORBIDDEN	asur	אָסוּר
NO TRESPASSING!	asur la'avor	אָסוּר לַעֲבוֹר
WET PAINT	'tseva lax	צֶבַע לַח

31. Shopping

to buy (purchase)	liknot	לִקְנוֹת
shopping	kniya	קְנִיָה (נ)
to go shopping	la'lexet lekniyot	לָלֶכֶת לִקְנִיוֹת
shopping	arixat kniyot	עֲרִיכַת קְנִיוֹת (נ)

| to be open (ab. shop) | pa'tuax | פָּתוּחַ |
| to be closed | sagur | סָגוּר |

footwear, shoes	na'a'layim	נַעֲלַיִים (נ"ר)
clothes, clothing	bgadim	בְּגָדִים (ז"ר)
cosmetics	tamrukim	תַּמְרוּקִים (ז"ר)
food products	mutsrei mazon	מוּצְרֵי מָזוֹן (ז"ר)
gift, present	matana	מַתָּנָה (נ)

| shop assistant (masc.) | moxer | מוֹכֵר (ז) |
| shop assistant (fem.) | mo'xeret | מוֹכֶרֶת (נ) |

| cash desk | kupa | קוּפָּה (נ) |
| mirror | mar'a | מַרְאָה (נ) |

counter (shop ~)	duχan	דּוּכָן (ז)
fitting room	'χeder halbaʃa	חֲדַר הַלְבָּשָׁה (ז)
to try on	limdod	לִמְדּוֹד
to fit (ab. dress, etc.)	lehat'im	לְהַתְאִים
to fancy (vt)	limtso χen be'ei'nayim	לִמְצוֹא חֵן בְּעֵינַיִים
price	meχir	מְחִיר (ז)
price tag	tag meχir	תַּג מְחִיר (ז)
to cost (vt)	la'alot	לַעֲלוֹת
How much?	'kama?	כַּמָה?
discount	hanaχa	הֲנָחָה (נ)
inexpensive (adj)	lo yakar	לֹא יָקָר
cheap (adj)	zol	זוֹל
expensive (adj)	yakar	יָקָר
It's expensive	ze yakar	זֶה יָקָר
hire (n)	haskara	הַשְׂכָּרָה (נ)
to hire (~ a dinner jacket)	liskor	לִשְׂכּוֹר
credit (trade credit)	aʃrai	אַשְׁרַאי (ז)
on credit (adv)	be'aʃrai	בְּאַשְׁרַאי

CLOTHING & ACCESSORIES

32. Outerwear. Coats

clothes	bgadim	בְּגָדִים (ז״ר)
outerwear	levuʃ elyon	לְבוּש עֶלְיוֹן (ז)
winter clothing	bigdei 'xoref	בִּגְדֵי חוֹרֶף (ז״ר)
coat (overcoat)	me'il	מְעִיל (ז)
fur coat	me'il parva	מְעִיל פַּרְוָוה (ז)
fur jacket	me'il parva katsar	מְעִיל פַּרְוָוה קָצָר (ז)
down coat	me'il pux	מְעִיל פּוּךְ (ז)
jacket (e.g. leather ~)	me'il katsar	מְעִיל קָצָר (ז)
raincoat (trenchcoat, etc.)	me'il 'geʃem	מְעִיל גֶּשֶׁם (ז)
waterproof (adj)	amid be'mayim	עָמִיד בְּמַיִם

33. Men's & women's clothing

shirt (button shirt)	xultsa	חוּלְצָה (נ)
trousers	mixna'sayim	מִכְנָסַיִים (ז״ר)
jeans	mixnesei 'dʒins	מִכְנְסֵי ג׳ִינְס (ז״ר)
suit jacket	ʒaket	ז׳ָקֵט (ז)
suit	xalifa	חֲלִיפָה (נ)
dress (frock)	simla	שִׂמְלָה (נ)
skirt	xatsa'it	חֲצָאִית (נ)
blouse	xultsa	חוּלְצָה (נ)
knitted jacket (cardigan, etc.)	ʒaket 'tsemer	ז׳ָקֵט צֶמֶר (ז)
jacket (of a woman's suit)	ʒaket	ז׳ָקֵט (ז)
T-shirt	ti ʃert	טִי שֶׁרְט (ז)
shorts (short trousers)	mixna'sayim ktsarim	מִכְנָסַיִים קְצָרִים (ז״ר)
tracksuit	'trening	טְרֶנִינְג (ז)
bathrobe	xaluk raxatsa	חָלוּק רַחְצָה (ז)
pyjamas	pi'dʒama	פִּיג׳ָמָה (נ)
jumper (sweater)	'sveder	סְוֶודֶר (ז)
pullover	afuda	אֲפוּדָה (נ)
waistcoat	vest	וֶסְט (ז)
tailcoat	frak	פְרָאק (ז)
dinner suit	tuk'sido	טוֹקְסִידוֹ (ז)
uniform	madim	מַדִים (ז״ר)
workwear	bigdei avoda	בִּגְדֵי עֲבוֹדָה (ז״ר)
boiler suit	sarbal	סַרְבָּל (ז)
coat (e.g. doctor's smock)	xaluk	חָלוּק (ז)

34. Clothing. Underwear

underwear	levanim	לְבָנִים (ז״ר)
pants	taxtonim	תַחְתוֹנִים (ז״ר)
panties	taxtonim	תַחְתוֹנִים (ז״ר)
vest (singlet)	gufiya	גוּפִיָּה (נ)
socks	gar'bayim	גַרְבַּיִם (ז״ר)
nightdress	'ktonet 'laila	כְּתוֹנֶת לַיְלָה (נ)
bra	xaziya	חֲזִיָּה (נ)
knee highs (knee-high socks)	birkon	בִּרְכּוֹן (ז)
tights	garbonim	גַרְבּוֹנִים (ז״ר)
stockings (hold ups)	garbei 'nailon	גַרְבֵּי נַיְלוֹן (ז״ר)
swimsuit, bikini	'beged yam	בֶּגֶד יָם (ז)

35. Headwear

hat	'kova	כּוֹבַע (ז)
trilby hat	'kova 'leved	כּוֹבַע לֶבֶד (ז)
baseball cap	'kova 'beisbol	כּוֹבַע בֵּייסְבּוֹל (ז)
flatcap	'kova mitsxiya	כּוֹבַע מִצְחִיָּה (ז)
beret	baret	בֶּרֶט (ז)
hood	bardas	בַּרְדָס (ז)
panama hat	'kova 'tembel	כּוֹבַע טֶמְבֶּל (ז)
knit cap (knitted hat)	'kova 'gerev	כּוֹבַע גֶרֶב (ז)
headscarf	mit'paxat	מִטְפַּחַת (נ)
women's hat	'kova	כּוֹבַע (ז)
hard hat	kasda	קַסְדָה (נ)
forage cap	kumta	כּוּמְתָה (נ)
helmet	kasda	קַסְדָה (נ)
bowler	mig'ba'at me'u'gelet	מִגְבַּעַת מְעוּגֶלֶת (נ)
top hat	tsi'linder	צִילִינְדֶר (ז)

36. Footwear

footwear	han'ala	הַנְעָלָה (נ)
shoes (men's shoes)	na'a'layim	נַעֲלַיִם (נ״ר)
shoes (women's shoes)	na'a'layim	נַעֲלַיִם (נ״ר)
boots (e.g., cowboy ~)	maga'fayim	מַגָפַיִם (ז״ר)
carpet slippers	na'alei 'bayit	נַעֲלֵי בַּיִת (נ״ר)
trainers	na'alei sport	נַעֲלֵי סְפּוֹרְט (נ״ר)
trainers	na'alei sport	נַעֲלֵי סְפּוֹרְט (נ״ר)
sandals	sandalim	סַנְדָלִים (ז״ר)
cobbler (shoe repairer)	sandlar	סַנְדְלָר (ז)
heel	akev	עָקֵב (ז)

pair (of shoes)	zug	זוּג (ז)
lace (shoelace)	sroχ	שְׂרוֹך (ז)
to lace up (vt)	lisroχ	לִשְׂרוֹך
shoehorn	kaf na'a'layim	כַּף נַעֲלַיִים (נ)
shoe polish	miʃχat na'a'layim	מִשְׁחַת נַעֲלַיִים (נ)

37. Personal accessories

gloves	kfafot	כְּפָפוֹת (נ"ר)
mittens	kfafot	כְּפָפוֹת (נ"ר)
scarf (muffler)	tsa'if	צָעִיף (ז)
glasses	miʃka'fayim	מִשְׁקָפַיִים (ז"ר)
frame (eyeglass ~)	mis'geret	מִסְגֶּרֶת (נ)
umbrella	mitriya	מְטְרִיָּה (נ)
walking stick	makel haliχa	מַקֵּל הֲלִיכָה (ז)
hairbrush	miv'reʃet se'ar	מִבְרֶשֶׁת שֵׂיעָר (נ)
fan	menifa	מְנִיפָה (נ)
tie (necktie)	aniva	עֲנִיבָה (נ)
bow tie	anivat parpar	עֲנִיבַת פַּרְפַּר (נ)
braces	ktefiyot	כְּתֵפִיּוֹת (נ"ר)
handkerchief	mimχata	מִמְחָטָה (נ)
comb	masrek	מַסְרֵק (ז)
hair slide	sikat roʃ	סִיכַּת רֹאשׁ (נ)
hairpin	sikat se'ar	סִיכַּת שֵׂיעָר (נ)
buckle	avzam	אַבְזָם (ז)
belt	χagora	חֲגוֹרָה (נ)
shoulder strap	retsu'at katef	רְצוּעַת כָּתֵף (נ)
bag (handbag)	tik	תִּיק (ז)
handbag	tik	תִּיק (ז)
rucksack	tarmil	תַּרְמִיל (ז)

38. Clothing. Miscellaneous

fashion	ofna	אוֹפְנָה (נ)
in vogue (adj)	ofnati	אוֹפְנָתִי
fashion designer	me'atsev ofna	מְעַצֵּב אוֹפְנָה (ז)
collar	tsavaron	צַוָּוארוֹן (ז)
pocket	kis	כִּיס (ז)
pocket (as adj)	ʃel kis	שֶׁל כִּיס
sleeve	ʃarvul	שַׁרווּל (ז)
hanging loop	mitle	מִתְלֶה (ז)
flies (on trousers)	χanut	חָנוּת (נ)
zip (fastener)	roχsan	רוֹכְסָן (ז)
fastener	'keres	קֶרֶס (ז)
button	kaftor	כַּפְתּוֹר (ז)

| buttonhole | lula'a | לוּלָאָה (נ) |
| to come off (ab. button) | lehitaleʃ | לְהִיתָלֵשׁ |

to sew (vi, vt)	litpor	לִתְפּוֹר
to embroider (vi, vt)	lirkom	לִרְקוֹם
embroidery	rikma	רִקְמָה (נ)
sewing needle	'maχat tfira	מַחַט תְּפִירָה (נ)
thread	χut	חוּט (ז)
seam	'tefer	תֶּפֶר (ז)

to get dirty (vi)	lehitlaχleχ	לְהִתְלַכְלֵךְ
stain (mark, spot)	'ketem	כֶּתֶם (ז)
to crease, to crumple	lehitkamet	לְהִתְקַמֵּט
to tear, to rip (vt)	lik'ro'a	לִקְרוֹעַ
clothes moth	aʃ	עָשׁ (ז)

39. Personal care. Cosmetics

toothpaste	miʃχat ʃi'nayim	מִשְׁחַת שִׁינַיִים (נ)
toothbrush	miv'reʃet ʃi'nayim	מִבְרֶשֶׁת שִׁינַיִים (נ)
to clean one's teeth	letsaχ'tseaχ ʃi'nayim	לְצַחְצֵחַ שִׁינַיִים

razor	'ta'ar	תַּעַר (ז)
shaving cream	'ketsef gi'luaχ	קֶצֶף גִּילוּחַ (ז)
to shave (vi)	lehitga'leaχ	לְהִתְגַּלֵּחַ

| soap | sabon | סַבּוֹן (ז) |
| shampoo | ʃampu | שַׁמְפּוּ (ז) |

scissors	mispa'rayim	מִסְפָּרַיִים (ז"ר)
nail file	ptsira	פְּצִירָה (נ)
nail clippers	gozez tsipor'nayim	גּוֹזֵז צִיפּוֹרְנַיִים (ז)
tweezers	pin'tseta	פִּינְצֶטָה (נ)

cosmetics	tamrukim	תַּמְרוּקִים (ז"ר)
face mask	maseχa	מַסֵכָה (נ)
manicure	manikur	מָנִיקוּר (ז)
to have a manicure	la'asot manikur	לַעֲשׂוֹת מָנִיקוּר
pedicure	pedikur	פֶּדִיקוּר (ז)

make-up bag	tik ipur	תִּיק אִיפּוּר (ז)
face powder	'pudra	פּוּדְרָה (נ)
powder compact	pudriya	פּוּדְרִיָּה (נ)
blusher	'somek	סוֹמֶק (ז)

perfume (bottled)	'bosem	בּוֹשֶׂם (ז)
toilet water (lotion)	mei 'bosem	מֵי בּוֹשֶׂם (ז"ר)
lotion	mei panim	מֵי פָּנִים (ז"ר)
cologne	mei 'bosem	מֵי בּוֹשֶׂם (ז"ר)

eyeshadow	tslalit	צְלָלִית (נ)
eyeliner	ai 'lainer	אַי לַיינֶר (ז)
mascara	'maskara	מַסְקָרָה (נ)
lipstick	sfaton	שְׁפָתוֹן (ז)

nail polish	'laka letsipor'nayim	לַקָּה לְצִיפּוֹרְנַיִים (נ)
hair spray	tarsis lese'ar	תַרְסִיס לְשֵׂיעָר (ז)
deodorant	de'odo'rant	דֵאוֹדוֹרַנְט (ז)
cream	krem	קְרֶם (ז)
face cream	krem panim	קְרֶם פָּנִים (ז)
hand cream	krem ya'dayim	קְרֶם יָדַיִים (ז)
anti-wrinkle cream	krem 'neged kmatim	קְרֶם נֶגֶד קְמָטִים (ז)
day cream	krem yom	קְרֶם יוֹם (ז)
night cream	krem 'laila	קְרֶם לַיְלָה (ז)
day (as adj)	yomi	יוֹמִי
night (as adj)	leili	לֵילִי
tampon	tampon	טַמְפּוֹן (ז)
toilet paper (toilet roll)	neyar tu'alet	נְיַיר טוֹאָלֶט (ז)
hair dryer	meyabef se'ar	מְיַיבֵּשׁ שֵׂיעָר (ז)

40. Watches. Clocks

watch (wristwatch)	ſe'on yad	שָׁעוֹן יָד (ז)
dial	'luaχ ſa'on	לוּחַ שָׁעוֹן (ז)
hand (clock, watch)	maχog	מָחוֹג (ז)
metal bracelet	tsamid	צָמִיד (ז)
watch strap	retsu'a leſa'on	רְצוּעָה לְשָׁעוֹן (נ)
battery	solela	סוֹלְלָה (נ)
to be flat (battery)	lehitroken	לְהִתְרוֹקֵן
to change a battery	lehaχlif	לְהַחְלִיף
to run fast	lemaher	לְמַהֵר
to run slow	lefager	לְפַגֵּר
wall clock	ſe'on kir	שָׁעוֹן קִיר (ז)
hourglass	ſe'on χol	שָׁעוֹן חוֹל (ז)
sundial	ſe'on 'ſemeſ	שָׁעוֹן שֶׁמֶשׁ (ז)
alarm clock	ſa'on me'orer	שָׁעוֹן מְעוֹרֵר (ז)
watchmaker	ſa'an	שָׁעָן (ז)
to repair (vt)	letaken	לְתַקֵּן

EVERYDAY EXPERIENCE

41. Money

money	'kesef	כֶּסֶף (ז)
currency exchange	hamara	הֲמָרָה (נ)
exchange rate	'ʃaʿar χalifin	שַׁעַר חֲלִיפִין (ז)
cashpoint	kaspomat	כַּספֹּומָט (ז)
coin	mat'beʿa	מַטבֵּעַ (ז)
dollar	'dolar	דֹולָר (ז)
euro	'eiro	אֵירֹו (ז)
lira	'lira	לִירָה (נ)
Deutschmark	mark germani	מַרק גֶּרמָנִי (ז)
franc	frank	פרַנק (ז)
pound sterling	'lira 'sterling	לִירָה שטֶרלִינג (נ)
yen	yen	יֶן (ז)
debt	χov	חֹוב (ז)
debtor	'baʿal χov	בַּעַל חֹוב (ז)
to lend (money)	lehalvot	לְהַלוֹות
to borrow (vi, vt)	lilvot	לִלוֹות
bank	bank	בַּנק (ז)
account	χeʃbon	חֶשבֹּון (ז)
to deposit (vt)	lehafkid	לְהַפקִיד
to deposit into the account	lehafkid leχeʃbon	לְהַפקִיד לְחֶשבֹּון
to withdraw (vt)	limʃoχ meχeʃbon	לִמשֹׁוך מֵחֶשבֹּון
credit card	kartis aʃrai	כַּרטִיס אַשרַאי (ז)
cash	mezuman	מְזוּמָן
cheque	tʃek	צֶ׳ק (ז)
to write a cheque	liχtov tʃek	לִכתֹּוב צֶ׳ק
chequebook	pinkas 'tʃekim	פִּנקָס צֶ׳קִים (ז)
wallet	arnak	אַרנָק (ז)
purse	arnak lematbe"ot	אַרנָק לְמַטבְּעֹות (ז)
safe	ka'sefet	כַּסֶפֶת (נ)
heir	yoreʃ	יֹורֵש (ז)
inheritance	yeruʃa	יְרוּשָׁה (נ)
fortune (wealth)	'oʃer	עֹושֶׁר (ז)
lease	χoze sχirut	חֹוזֶה שׂכִירוּת (ז)
rent (money)	sχar dira	שׂכַר דִּירָה (ז)
to rent (sth from sb)	liskor	לִשׂכֹּור
price	meχir	מְחִיר (ז)
cost	alut	עֲלוּת (נ)

47

sum	sχum	סכום (ז)
to spend (vt)	lehoţsi	לְהוֹצִיא
expenses	hotsa'ot	הוֹצָאוֹת (נ"ר)
to economize (vi, vt)	laχasoχ	לַחֲסוֹך
economical	χesχoni	חֶסְכוֹנִי

to pay (vi, vt)	leʃalem	לְשַׁלֵם
payment	taʃlum	תַשְׁלוּם (ז)
change (give the ~)	'odef	עוֹדֶף (ז)

tax	mas	מַס (ז)
fine	knas	קְנָס (ז)
to fine (vt)	liknos	לִקְנוֹס

42. Post. Postal service

post office	'do'ar	דוֹאַר (ז)
post (letters, etc.)	'do'ar	דוֹאַר (ז)
postman	davar	דַוָּור (ז)
opening hours	ʃa'ot avoda	שְׁעוֹת עֲבוֹדָה (נ"ר)

letter	miχtav	מִכְתָב (ז)
registered letter	miχtav raʃum	מִכְתָב רָשׁוּם (ז)
postcard	gluya	גְלוּיָה (נ)
telegram	mivrak	מִבְרָק (ז)
parcel	χavila	חֲבִילָה (נ)
money transfer	ha'avarat ksafim	הַעֲבָרַת כְּסָפִים (נ)

to receive (vt)	lekabel	לְקַבֵּל
to send (vt)	liʃ'loaχ	לִשְׁלוֹחַ
sending	ʃliχa	שְׁלִיחָה (ז)
address	'ktovet	כְּתוֹבֶת (נ)
postcode	mikud	מִיקוּד (ז)
sender	ʃo'leaχ	שׁוֹלֵחַ (ז)
receiver	nim'an	נִמְעָן (ז)

name (first name)	ʃem prati	שֵׁם פְּרָטִי (ז)
surname (last name)	ʃem miʃpaχa	שֵׁם מִשְׁפָּחָה (ז)
postage rate	ta'arif	תַעֲרִיף (ז)
standard (adj)	ragil	רָגִיל
economical (adj)	χesχoni	חֶסְכוֹנִי

weight	miʃkal	מִשְׁקָל (ז)
to weigh (~ letters)	liʃkol	לִשְׁקוֹל
envelope	ma'atafa	מַעֲטָפָה (נ)
postage stamp	bul 'do'ar	בּוּל דוֹאַר (ז)
to stamp an envelope	lehadbik bul	לְהַדְבִּיק בּוּל

43. Banking

| bank | bank | בַּנְק (ז) |
| branch (of a bank) | snif | סְנִיף (ז) |

consultant	yo'ets	יוֹעֵץ (ז)
manager (director)	menahel	מְנַהֵל (ז)
bank account	xeʃbon	חֶשְׁבּוֹן (ז)
account number	mispar xeʃbon	מִסְפַּר חֶשְׁבּוֹן (ז)
current account	xeʃbon over vaʃav	חֶשְׁבּוֹן עוֹבֵר וָשָׁב (ז)
deposit account	xeʃbon xisaxon	חֶשְׁבּוֹן חִסָּכוֹן (ז)
to open an account	liftoax xeʃbon	לִפְתּוֹחַ חֶשְׁבּוֹן
to close the account	lisgor xeʃbon	לִסְגּוֹר חֶשְׁבּוֹן
to deposit into the account	lehafkid lexeʃbon	לְהַפְקִיד לְחֶשְׁבּוֹן
to withdraw (vt)	limʃox mexeʃbon	לִמְשׁוֹך מֵחֶשְׁבּוֹן
deposit	pikadon	פִּיקָדוֹן (ז)
to make a deposit	lehafkid	לְהַפְקִיד
wire transfer	ha'avara banka'it	הַעֲבָרָה בַּנְקָאִית (נ)
to wire, to transfer	leha'avir 'kesef	לְהַעֲבִיר כֶּסֶף
sum	sxum	סְכוּם (ז)
How much?	'kama?	כַּמָּה?
signature	xatima	חֲתִימָה (נ)
to sign (vt)	laxtom	לַחְתּוֹם
credit card	kartis aʃrai	כַּרְטִיס אַשְׁרַאי (ז)
code (PIN code)	kod	קוֹד (ז)
credit card number	mispar kartis aʃrai	מִסְפַּר כַּרְטִיס אַשְׁרַאי (ז)
cashpoint	kaspomat	כַּסְפּוֹמָט (ז)
cheque	tʃek	צֶ'ק (ז)
to write a cheque	lixtov tʃek	לִכְתּוֹב צֶ'ק
chequebook	pinkas 'tʃekim	פִּנְקַס צֶ'קִים (ז)
loan (bank ~)	halva'a	הַלְוָאָה (נ)
to apply for a loan	levakeʃ halva'a	לְבַקֵּשׁ הַלְוָאָה
to get a loan	lekabel halva'a	לְקַבֵּל הַלְוָאָה
to give a loan	lehalvot	לְהַלְווֹת
guarantee	arvut	עַרְבוּת (נ)

44. Telephone. Phone conversation

telephone	'telefon	טֶלֶפוֹן (ז)
mobile phone	'telefon nayad	טֶלֶפוֹן נַיָּיד (ז)
answerphone	meʃivon	מְשִׁיבוֹן (ז)
to call (by phone)	letsaltsel	לְצַלְצֵל
call, ring	sixat 'telefon	שִׂיחַת טֶלֶפוֹן (נ)
to dial a number	lexayeg mispar	לְחַיֵּיג מִסְפָּר
Hello!	'halo!	הָלוֹ!
to ask (vt)	liʃol	לִשְׁאוֹל
to answer (vi, vt)	la'anot	לַעֲנוֹת
to hear (vt)	liʃmo'a	לִשְׁמוֹעַ
well (adv)	tov	טוֹב

not well (adv)	lo tov	לֹא טוֹב
noises (interference)	hafra'ot	הַפְרָעוֹת (נ״ר)
receiver	ʃfo'feret	שְׁפוֹפֶרֶת (נ)
to pick up (~ the phone)	leharim ʃfo'feret	לְהָרִים שְׁפוֹפֶרֶת
to hang up (~ the phone)	leha'niaχ ʃfo'feret	לְהָנִיחַ שְׁפוֹפֶרֶת
busy (engaged)	tafus	תָּפוּס
to ring (ab. phone)	letsaltsel	לְצַלְצֵל
telephone book	'sefer tele'fonim	סֵפֶר טֶלֶפוֹנִים (ז)
local (adj)	mekomi	מְקוֹמִי
local call	siχa mekomit	שִׂיחָה מְקוֹמִית (נ)
trunk (e.g. ~ call)	bein ironi	בֵּין עִירוֹנִי
trunk call	siχa bein ironit	שִׂיחָה בֵּין עִירוֹנִית (נ)
international (adj)	benle'umi	בֵּינלְאוּמִי
international call	siχa benle'umit	שִׂיחָה בֵּינלְאוּמִית (נ)

45. Mobile telephone

mobile phone	'telefon nayad	טֶלֶפוֹן נַיָּד (ז)
display	masaχ	מָסָךְ (ז)
button	kaftor	כַּפְתּוֹר (ז)
SIM card	kartis sim	כַּרְטִיס סִים (ז)
battery	solela	סוֹלְלָה (נ)
to be flat (battery)	lehitroken	לְהִתְרוֹקֵן
charger	mit'an	מַטְעָן (ז)
menu	tafrit	תַּפְרִיט (ז)
settings	hagdarot	הַגְדָּרוֹת (נ״ר)
tune (melody)	mangina	מַנְגִּינָה (נ)
to select (vt)	livχor	לִבְחוֹר
calculator	maxʃevon	מַחְשְׁבוֹן (ז)
voice mail	ta koli	תָּא קוֹלִי (ז)
alarm clock	ʃa'on me'orer	שְׁעוֹן מְעוֹרֵר (ז)
contacts	anʃei 'keʃer	אַנְשֵׁי קֶשֶׁר (ז״ר)
SMS (text message)	misron	מִסְרוֹן (ז)
subscriber	manui	מָנוּי (ז)

46. Stationery

ballpoint pen	et kaduri	עֵט כַּדּוּרִי (ז)
fountain pen	et no've'a	עֵט נוֹבֵעַ (ז)
pencil	iparon	עִיפָּרוֹן (ז)
highlighter	'marker	מַרְקֵר (ז)
felt-tip pen	tuʃ	טוּשׁ (ז)
notepad	pinkas	פִּנְקָס (ז)
diary	yoman	יוֹמָן (ז)

ruler	sargel	סַרְגֵּל (ז)
calculator	maxʃevon	מַחְשְׁבוֹן (ז)
rubber	'maxak	מָחַק (ז)
drawing pin	'na'ats	נַעַץ (ז)
paper clip	mehadek	מְהַדֵּק (ז)
glue	'devek	דֶּבֶק (ז)
stapler	ʃadxan	שַׁדְכָן (ז)
hole punch	menakev	מְנַקֵּב (ז)
pencil sharpener	maxded	מַחְדֵּד (ז)

47. Foreign languages

language	safa	שָׂפָה (נ)
foreign (adj)	zar	זָר
foreign language	safa zara	שָׂפָה זָרָה (נ)
to study (vt)	lilmod	לִלְמוֹד
to learn (language, etc.)	lilmod	לִלְמוֹד
to read (vi, vt)	likro	לִקְרוֹא
to speak (vi, vt)	ledaber	לְדַבֵּר
to understand (vt)	lehavin	לְהָבִין
to write (vt)	lixtov	לִכְתּוֹב
fast (adv)	maher	מַהֵר
slowly (adv)	le'at	לְאַט
fluently (adv)	xofʃi	חוֹפְשִׁי
rules	klalim	כְּלָלִים (ז"ר)
grammar	dikduk	דִּקְדּוּק (ז)
vocabulary	otsar milim	אוֹצַר מִילִים (ז)
phonetics	torat ha'hege	תּוֹרַת הַהֶגֶה (נ)
textbook	'sefer limud	סֵפֶר לִימוּד (ז)
dictionary	milon	מִילוֹן (ז)
teach-yourself book	'sefer lelimud atsmi	סֵפֶר לְלִימוּד עַצְמִי (ז)
phrasebook	sixon	שִׂיחוֹן (ז)
cassette, tape	ka'letet	קַלֶּטֶת (נ)
videotape	ka'letet 'vide'o	קַלֶּטֶת וִידֵיאוֹ (נ)
CD, compact disc	taklitor	תַּקְלִיטוֹר (ז)
DVD	di vi di	דִי. וִי. דִי. (ז)
alphabet	alefbeit	אָלֶפְבֵּית (ז)
to spell (vt)	le'ayet	לְאַיֵּת
pronunciation	hagiya	הֲגִייָה (נ)
accent	mivta	מִבְטָא (ז)
with an accent	im mivta	עִם מִבְטָא
without an accent	bli mivta	בְּלִי מִבְטָא
word	mila	מִילָה (נ)
meaning	maʃma'ut	מַשְׁמָעוּת (נ)
course (e.g. a French ~)	kurs	קוּרְס (ז)

to sign up	leherafem lekurs	לְהֵירָשֵׁם לְקוּרס
teacher	more	מוֹרָה (ז)
translation (process)	tirgum	תַרגוּם (ז)
translation (text, etc.)	tirgum	תַרגוּם (ז)
translator	metargem	מְתַרגֵם (ז)
interpreter	meturgeman	מְתוּרגְמָן (ז)
polyglot	poliglot	פּוֹלִיגלוֹט (ז)
memory	zikaron	זִיכָּרוֹן (ז)

MEALS. RESTAURANT

48. Table setting

spoon	kaf	כַּף (ז)
knife	sakin	סַכִּין (ז, נ)
fork	mazleg	מַזְלֵג (ז)
cup (e.g., coffee ~)	'sefel	סֵפֶל (ז)
plate (dinner ~)	tsa'laxat	צַלַּחַת (נ)
saucer	taxtit	תַּחְתִּית (נ)
serviette	mapit	מַפִּית (נ)
toothpick	keisam ʃi'nayim	קִיסָם שִׁנַּיִם (ז)

49. Restaurant

restaurant	mis'ada	מִסְעָדָה (נ)
coffee bar	beit kafe	בֵּית קָפֶה (ז)
pub, bar	bar, pab	בָּר, פָּאב (ז)
tearoom	beit te	בֵּית תֶּה (ז)
waiter	meltsar	מֶלְצַר (ז)
waitress	meltsarit	מֶלְצָרִית (נ)
barman	'barmen	בַּרְמֶן (ז)
menu	tafrit	תַּפְרִיט (ז)
wine list	reʃimat yeynot	רְשִׁימַת יֵינוֹת (נ)
to book a table	lehazmin ʃulxan	לְהַזְמִין שׁוּלְחָן
course, dish	mana	מָנָה (נ)
to order (meal)	lehazmin	לְהַזְמִין
to make an order	lehazmin	לְהַזְמִין
aperitif	maʃke meta'aven	מַשְׁקֶה מְתַאָבֵן (ז)
starter	meta'aven	מְתַאָבֵן (ז)
dessert, pudding	ki'nuax	קִינוּחַ (ז)
bill	xeʃbon	חֶשְׁבּוֹן (ז)
to pay the bill	leʃalem	לְשַׁלֵּם
to give change	latet 'odef	לָתֵת עוֹדֶף
tip	tip	טִיפ (ז)

50. Meals

food	'oxel	אוֹכֶל (ז)
to eat (vi, vt)	le'exol	לֶאֱכוֹל

breakfast	aruxat 'boker	אֲרוּחַת בּוֹקֶר (נ)
to have breakfast	le'exol aruxat 'boker	לֶאֱכֹל אֲרוּחַת בּוֹקֶר
lunch	aruxat tsaha'rayim	אֲרוּחַת צָהֳרַיִים (נ)
to have lunch	le'exol aruxat tsaha'rayim	לֶאֱכֹל אֲרוּחַת צָהֳרַיִים
dinner	aruxat 'erev	אֲרוּחַת עֶרֶב (נ)
to have dinner	le'exol aruxat 'erev	לֶאֱכֹל אֲרוּחַת עֶרֶב
appetite	te'avon	תֵּיאָבוֹן (ז)
Enjoy your meal!	betei'avon!	בְּתֵיאָבוֹן!
to open (~ a bottle)	lif'toax	לִפְתּוֹחַ
to spill (liquid)	liʃpox	לִשְׁפּוֹךְ
to spill out (vi)	lehiʃapex	לְהִישָׁפֵךְ
to boil (vi)	lir'toax	לִרְתּוֹחַ
to boil (vt)	lehar'tiax	לְהַרְתִּיחַ
boiled (~ water)	ra'tuax	רָתוּחַ
to chill, cool down (vt)	lekarer	לְקָרֵר
to chill (vi)	lehitkarer	לְהִתְקָרֵר
taste, flavour	'ta'am	טַעַם (ז)
aftertaste	'ta'am levai	טַעַם לְווַאי (ז)
to slim down (lose weight)	lirzot	לִרְזוֹת
diet	di''eta	דִּיאָטָה (נ)
vitamin	vitamin	וִיטָמִין (ז)
calorie	ka'lorya	קָלוֹרְיָה (נ)
vegetarian (n)	tsimxoni	צִמְחוֹנִי (ז)
vegetarian (adj)	tsimxoni	צִמְחוֹנִי
fats (nutrient)	ʃumanim	שׁוּמָנִים (ז"ר)
proteins	xelbonim	חֶלְבּוֹנִים (ז"ר)
carbohydrates	paxmema	פַּחְמֵימָה (נ)
slice (of lemon, ham)	prusa	פְּרוּסָה (נ)
piece (of cake, pie)	xatixa	חֲתִיכָה (נ)
crumb (of bread, cake, etc.)	perur	פֵּירוּר (ז)

51. Cooked dishes

course, dish	mana	מָנָה (נ)
cuisine	mitbax	מִטְבָּח (ז)
recipe	matkon	מַתְכּוֹן (ז)
portion	mana	מָנָה (נ)
salad	salat	סָלָט (ז)
soup	marak	מָרָק (ז)
clear soup (broth)	marak tsax, tsir	מָרָק צַח, צִיר (ז)
sandwich (bread)	karix	כָּרִיךְ (ז)
fried eggs	beitsat ain	בֵּיצַת עַיִן (נ)
hamburger (beefburger)	'hamburger	הַמְבּוּרְגֶּר (ז)
beefsteak	umtsa, steik	אוּמְצָה (נ), סְטֵייק (ז)
side dish	to'sefet	תּוֹסֶפֶת (נ)

spaghetti	spa'geti	סְפָּגֶטִי (ז)
mash	meχit tapuχei adama	מְחִית תַּפּוּחֵי אֲדָמָה (נ)
pizza	'pitsa	פִּיצָה (נ)
porridge (oatmeal, etc.)	daysa	דַּיְסָה (נ)
omelette	χavita	חֲבִיתָה (נ)

boiled (e.g. ~ beef)	mevuʃal	מְבוּשָׁל
smoked (adj)	me'uʃan	מְעוּשָׁן
fried (adj)	metugan	מְטוּגָּן
dried (adj)	meyubaʃ	מְיוּבָּשׁ
frozen (adj)	kafu	קָפוּא
pickled (adj)	kavuʃ	כָּבוּשׁ

sweet (sugary)	matok	מָתוֹק
salty (adj)	ma'luaχ	מָלוּחַ
cold (adj)	kar	קַר
hot (adj)	χam	חַם
bitter (adj)	marir	מָרִיר
tasty (adj)	ta'im	טָעִים

to cook in boiling water	levaʃel be'mayim rotχim	לְבַשֵּׁל בְּמַיִם רוֹתְחִים
to cook (dinner)	levaʃel	לְבַשֵּׁל
to fry (vt)	letagen	לְטַגֵּן
to heat up (food)	leχamem	לְחַמֵּם

to salt (vt)	leham'liaχ	לְהַמְלִיחַ
to pepper (vt)	lefalpel	לְפַלְפֵּל
to grate (vt)	lerasek	לְרַסֵּק
peel (n)	klipa	קְלִיפָּה (נ)
to peel (vt)	lekalef	לְקַלֵּף

52. Food

meat	basar	בָּשָׂר (ז)
chicken	of	עוֹף (ז)
poussin	pargit	פַּרְגִּית (נ)
duck	barvaz	בַּרְוָז (ז)
goose	avaz	אַוָּז (ז)
game	'tsayid	צַיִד (ז)
turkey	'hodu	הוֹדוּ (ז)

pork	basar χazir	בָּשָׂר חֲזִיר (ז)
veal	basar 'egel	בָּשָׂר עֵגֶל (ז)
lamb	basar 'keves	בָּשָׂר כֶּבֶשׂ (ז)
beef	bakar	בָּקָר (ז)
rabbit	arnav	אַרְנָב (ז)

sausage (bologna, etc.)	naknik	נַקְנִיק (ז)
vienna sausage (frankfurter)	naknikiya	נַקְנִיקִיָּיה (נ)
bacon	'kotel χazir	קוֹתֶל חֲזִיר (ז)
ham	basar χazir me'uʃan	בָּשָׂר חֲזִיר מְעוּשָׁן (ז)
gammon	'kotel χazir me'uʃan	קוֹתֶל חֲזִיר מְעוּשָׁן (ז)
pâté	pate	פָּטֶה (ז)
liver	kaved	כָּבֵד (ז)

mince (minced meat)	basar taχun	בָּשָׂר טָחוּן (ז)
tongue	laʃon	לָשׁוֹן (נ)
egg	beitsa	בֵּיצָה (נ)
eggs	beitsim	בֵּיצִים (נ״ר)
egg white	χelbon	חֶלְבּוֹן (ז)
egg yolk	χelmon	חֶלְמוֹן (ז)
fish	dag	דָּג (ז)
seafood	perot yam	פֵּירוֹת יָם (ז״ר)
crustaceans	sartana'im	סַרְטָנָאִים (ז״ר)
caviar	kavyar	קָוְויָאר (ז)
crab	sartan yam	סַרְטָן יָם (ז)
prawn	ʃrimps	שְׁרִימְפְּס (ז״ר)
oyster	tsidpat ma'aχal	צִדְפַּת מַאֲכָל (נ)
spiny lobster	'lobster kotsani	לוֹבְּסְטֶר קוֹצָנִי (ז)
octopus	tamnun	תַּמְנוּן (ז)
squid	kala'mari	קָלָמָארִי (ז)
sturgeon	basar haχidkan	בָּשָׂר הַחִדְקָן (ז)
salmon	'salmon	סַלְמוֹן (ז)
halibut	putit	פּוּטִית (נ)
cod	ʃibut	שִׁיבּוּט (ז)
mackerel	kolyas	קוֹלְיַס (ז)
tuna	'tuna	טוּנָה (נ)
eel	tslofaχ	צְלוֹפָח (ז)
trout	forel	פוֹרֵל (ז)
sardine	sardin	סַרְדִּין (ז)
pike	ze'ev 'mayim	זְאֵב מַיִם (ז)
herring	ma'liaχ	מָלִיחַ (ז)
bread	'leχem	לֶחֶם (ז)
cheese	gvina	גְּבִינָה (נ)
sugar	sukar	סוּכָּר (ז)
salt	'melaχ	מֶלַח (ז)
rice	'orez	אוֹרֶז (ז)
pasta (macaroni)	'pasta	פַּסְטָה (נ)
noodles	irtiyot	אִטְרִיּוֹת (נ״ר)
butter	χem'a	חֶמְאָה (נ)
vegetable oil	'ʃemen tsimχi	שֶׁמֶן צִמְחִי (ז)
sunflower oil	'ʃemen χamaniyot	שֶׁמֶן חַמָּנִיּוֹת (ז)
margarine	marga'rina	מַרְגָּרִינָה (נ)
olives	zeitim	זֵיתִים (ז״ר)
olive oil	'ʃemen 'zayit	שֶׁמֶן זַיִת (ז)
milk	χalav	חָלָב (ז)
condensed milk	χalav merukaz	חָלָב מְרוּכָּז (ז)
yogurt	'yogurt	יוֹגוּרְט (ז)
soured cream	ʃa'menet	שַׁמֶּנֶת (נ)
cream (of milk)	ʃa'menet	שַׁמֶּנֶת (נ)

mayonnaise	mayonez	מָיוֹנֵז (ז)
buttercream	ka'tsefet χem'a	קַצֶּפֶת חֶמְאָה (נ)
groats (barley ~, etc.)	grisim	גְּרִיסִים (ז"ר)
flour	'kemaχ	קֶמַח (ז)
tinned food	ʃimurim	שִׁימוּרִים (ז"ר)
cornflakes	ptitei 'tiras	פְּתִיתֵי תִּירָס (ז"ר)
honey	dvaʃ	דְּבַשׁ (ז)
jam	riba	רִיבָּה (נ)
chewing gum	'mastik	מַסְטִיק (ז)

53. Drinks

water	'mayim	מַיִם (ז"ר)
drinking water	mei ʃtiya	מֵי שתִיָּה (ז"ר)
mineral water	'mayim mine'raliyim	מַיִם מִינֶרָלִיִּים (ז"ר)
still (adj)	lo mugaz	לֹא מוּגָז
carbonated (adj)	mugaz	מוּגָז
sparkling (adj)	mugaz	מוּגָז
ice	'keraχ	קֶרַח (ז)
with ice	im 'keraχ	עִם קֶרַח
non-alcoholic (adj)	natul alkohol	נָטוּל אַלכּוֹהוֹל
soft drink	maʃke kal	מַשׁקֶה קַל (ז)
refreshing drink	maʃke mera'anen	מַשׁקֶה מְרַעֲנֵן (ז)
lemonade	limo'nada	לִימוֹנָדָה (נ)
spirits	maʃka'ot χarifim	מַשׁקָאוֹת חָרִיפִים (ז"ר)
wine	'yayin	יַיִן (ז)
white wine	'yayin lavan	יַיִן לָבָן (ז)
red wine	'yayin adom	יַיִן אָדֹם (ז)
liqueur	liker	לִיקֶר (ז)
champagne	ʃam'panya	שַׁמְפַּנְיָה (נ)
vermouth	'vermut	וֶרְמוּט (ז)
whisky	'viski	וִיסְקִי (ז)
vodka	'vodka	וֹדְקָה (נ)
gin	dʒin	גִ'ין (ז)
cognac	'konyak	קוֹנְיַאק (ז)
rum	rom	רוֹם (ז)
coffee	kafe	קָפֶּה (ז)
black coffee	kafe ʃaχor	קָפֶּה שָׁחוֹר (ז)
white coffee	kafe hafuχ	קָפֶּה הָפוּך (ז)
cappuccino	kapu'tʃino	קָפוּצִ'ינוֹ (ז)
instant coffee	kafe names	קָפֶּה נָמֵס (ז)
milk	χalav	חָלָב (ז)
cocktail	kokteil	קוֹקְטֵיל (ז)
milkshake	'milkʃeik	מִילקְשֵׁייק (ז)
juice	mits	מִיץ (ז)

tomato juice	mits agvaniyot	מִיץ עַגְבָנִיּוֹת (ז)
orange juice	mits tapuzim	מִיץ תַּפּוּזִים (ז)
freshly squeezed juice	mits saχut	מִיץ סָחוּט (ז)
beer	'bira	בִּירָה (נ)
lager	'bira bahira	בִּירָה בָּהִירָה (נ)
bitter	'bira keha	בִּירָה כֵּהָה (נ)
tea	te	תֵּה (ז)
black tea	te ʃaχor	תֵּה שָׁחוֹר (ז)
green tea	te yarok	תֵּה יָרוֹק (ז)

54. Vegetables

vegetables	yerakot	יְרָקוֹת (ז"ר)
greens	'yerek	יָרָק (ז)
tomato	agvaniya	עַגְבָנִיָּה (נ)
cucumber	melafefon	מְלָפְפוֹן (ז)
carrot	'gezer	גֶּזֶר (ז)
potato	ta'puaχ adama	תַּפּוּחַ אֲדָמָה (ז)
onion	batsal	בָּצָל (ז)
garlic	ʃum	שׁוּם (ז)
cabbage	kruv	כְּרוּב (ז)
cauliflower	kruvit	כְּרוּבִית (נ)
Brussels sprouts	kruv nitsanim	כְּרוּב נִצָּנִים (ז)
broccoli	'brokoli	בְּרוֹקוֹלִי (ז)
beetroot	'selek	סֶלֶק (ז)
aubergine	χatsil	חָצִיל (ז)
courgette	kiʃu	קִישׁוּא (ז)
pumpkin	'dla'at	דְּלַעַת (נ)
turnip	'lefet	לֶפֶת (נ)
parsley	petro'zilya	פֶּטְרוֹזִילְיָה (נ)
dill	ʃamir	שָׁמִיר (ז)
lettuce	'χasa	חַסָּה (נ)
celery	'seleri	סֶלֶרִי (ז)
asparagus	aspa'ragos	אַסְפָּרָגּוֹס (ז)
spinach	'tered	תֶּרֶד (ז)
pea	afuna	אֲפוּנָה (נ)
beans	pol	פּוֹל (ז)
maize	'tiras	תִּירָס (ז)
kidney bean	ʃu'it	שְׁעוּעִית (נ)
sweet paper	'pilpel	פִּלְפֵּל (ז)
radish	tsnonit	צְנוֹנִית (נ)
artichoke	artiʃok	אַרְטִישׁוֹק (ז)

55. Fruits. Nuts

fruit	pri	פְּרִי (ז)
apple	ta'puaχ	תַּפּוּחַ (ז)
pear	agas	אַגָּס (ז)
lemon	limon	לִימוֹן (ז)
orange	tapuz	תַּפּוּז (ז)
strawberry (garden ~)	tut sade	תּוּת שָׂדֶה (ז)
tangerine	klemen'tina	קְלֶמֶנְטִינָה (נ)
plum	ʃezif	שְׁזִיף (ז)
peach	afarsek	אֲפַרְסֵק (ז)
apricot	'miʃmeʃ	מִשְׁמֵשׁ (ז)
raspberry	'petel	פֶּטֶל (ז)
pineapple	'ananas	אֲנָנָס (ז)
banana	ba'nana	בַּנָּנָה (נ)
watermelon	ava'tiaχ	אֲבַטִּיחַ (ז)
grape	anavim	עֲנָבִים (ז"ר)
sour cherry	duvdevan	דּוּבְדְּבָן (ז)
sweet cherry	gudgedan	גּוּדְגְּדָן (ז)
melon	melon	מֶלוֹן (ז)
grapefruit	eʃkolit	אֶשְׁכּוֹלִית (נ)
avocado	avo'kado	אָבוֹקָדוֹ (ז)
papaya	pa'paya	פָּפָּאיָה (נ)
mango	'mango	מַנְגּוֹ (ז)
pomegranate	rimon	רִימּוֹן (ז)
redcurrant	dumdemanit aduma	דּוּמְדְּמָנִית אֲדוּמָה (נ)
blackcurrant	dumdemanit ʃχora	דּוּמְדְּמָנִית שְׁחוֹרָה (נ)
gooseberry	χazarzar	חֲזַרְזָר (ז)
bilberry	uχmanit	אוּכְמָנִית (נ)
blackberry	'petel ʃaχor	פֶּטֶל שָׁחוֹר (ז)
raisin	tsimukim	צִימוּקִים (ז"ר)
fig	te'ena	תְּאֵנָה (נ)
date	tamar	תָּמָר (ז)
peanut	botnim	בּוֹטְנִים (ז"ר)
almond	ʃaked	שָׁקֵד (ז)
walnut	egoz 'meleχ	אֱגוֹז מֶלֶךְ (ז)
hazelnut	egoz ilsar	אֱגוֹז אִלְסָר (ז)
coconut	'kokus	קוֹקוּס (ז)
pistachios	'fistuk	פִּיסְטוּק (ז)

56. Bread. Sweets

bakers' confectionery (pastry)	mutsrei kondi'torya	מוּצְרֵי קוֹנְדִיטוֹרְיָה (ז"ר)
bread	'leχem	לֶחֶם (ז)
biscuits	ugiya	עוּגִיָּה (נ)
chocolate (n)	'ʃokolad	שׁוֹקוֹלָד (ז)
chocolate (as adj)	mi'ʃokolad	מְשׁוֹקוֹלָד

candy (wrapped)	sukariya	סֻכָּרִיָּה (נ)
cake (e.g. cupcake)	uga	עוּגָה (נ)
cake (e.g. birthday ~)	uga	עוּגָה (נ)
pie (e.g. apple ~)	pai	פַּאי (ז)
filling (for cake, pie)	milui	מִילוּי (ז)
jam (whole fruit jam)	riba	רִיבָּה (נ)
marmalade	marme'lada	מַרְמָלָדָה (נ)
wafers	'vaflim	וָפְלִים (ז"ר)
ice-cream	'glida	גְלִידָה (נ)
pudding (Christmas ~)	'puding	פּוּדִינג (ז)

57. Spices

salt	'melaχ	מֶלַח (ז)
salty (adj)	ma'luaχ	מָלוּחַ
to salt (vt)	leham'liaχ	לְהַמְלִיחַ
black pepper	'pilpel ʃaχor	פִּלְפֵּל שָׁחוֹר (ז)
red pepper (milled ~)	'pilpel adom	פִּלְפֵּל אָדוֹם (ז)
mustard	χardal	חַרְדָל (ז)
horseradish	χa'zeret	חֲזֶרֶת (נ)
condiment	'rotev	רוֹטֶב (ז)
spice	tavlin	תַבְלִין (ז)
sauce	'rotev	רוֹטֶב (ז)
vinegar	'χomets	חוֹמֶץ (ז)
anise	kamnon	כַּמְנוֹן (ז)
basil	reχan	רֵיחָן (ז)
cloves	tsi'poren	צִיפּוֹרֶן (ז)
ginger	'dʒindʒer	גִ׳ינגֶ׳ר (ז)
coriander	'kusbara	כּוּסְבָּרָה (נ)
cinnamon	kinamon	קִינָמוֹן (ז)
sesame	'ʃumʃum	שׁוּמְשׁוֹם (ז)
bay leaf	ale dafna	עֲלֵה דַפְנָה (ז)
paprika	'paprika	פַּפְרִיקָה (נ)
caraway	'kimel	קִימֶל (ז)
saffron	ze'afran	זַעֲפְרָן (ז)

PERSONAL INFORMATION. FAMILY

58. Personal information. Forms

name (first name)	ʃem	שֵׁם (ז)
surname (last name)	ʃem miʃpaχa	שֵׁם מִשְׁפָּחָה (ז)
date of birth	ta'ariχ leda	תַּאֲרִיךְ לֵידָה (ז)
place of birth	mekom leda	מְקוֹם לֵידָה (ז)
nationality	le'om	לְאוֹם (ז)
place of residence	mekom megurim	מְקוֹם מְגוּרִים (ז)
country	medina	מְדִינָה (נ)
profession (occupation)	mik'tso'a	מִקְצוֹעַ (ז)
gender, sex	min	מִין (ז)
height	'gova	גּוֹבַה (ז)
weight	miʃkal	מִשְׁקָל (ז)

59. Family members. Relatives

mother	em	אֵם (נ)
father	av	אָב (ז)
son	ben	בֵּן (ז)
daughter	bat	בַּת (נ)
younger daughter	habat haktana	הַבַּת הַקְּטַנָּה (נ)
younger son	haben hakatan	הַבֵּן הַקָּטָן (ז)
eldest daughter	habat habχora	הַבַּת הַבְּכוֹרָה (נ)
eldest son	haben habχor	הַבֵּן הַבְּכוֹר (ז)
brother	aχ	אָח (ז)
elder brother	aχ gadol	אָח גָּדוֹל (ז)
younger brother	aχ katan	אָח קָטָן (ז)
sister	aχot	אָחוֹת (נ)
elder sister	aχot gdola	אָחוֹת גְדוֹלָה (נ)
younger sister	aχot ktana	אָחוֹת קְטַנָּה (נ)
cousin (masc.)	ben dod	בֵּן דוֹד (ז)
cousin (fem.)	bat 'doda	בַּת דּוֹדָה (נ)
mummy	'ima	אִמָּא (נ)
dad, daddy	'aba	אַבָּא (ז)
parents	horim	הוֹרִים (ז"ר)
child	'yeled	יֶלֶד (ז)
children	yeladim	יְלָדִים (ז"ר)
grandmother	'savta	סָבְתָא (נ)
grandfather	'saba	סָבָּא (ז)
grandson	'neχed	נֶכֶד (ז)

granddaughter	neχda	נֶכְדָּה (נ)
grandchildren	neχadim	נְכָדִים (ז"ר)
uncle	dod	דּוֹד (ז)
aunt	'doda	דּוֹדָה (נ)
nephew	aχyan	אַחְיָן (ז)
niece	aχyanit	אַחְיָנִית (נ)
mother-in-law (wife's mother)	χamot	חָמוֹת (נ)
father-in-law (husband's father)	χam	חָם (ז)
son-in-law (daughter's husband)	χatan	חָתָן (ז)
stepmother	em χoreget	אֵם חוֹרֶגֶת (נ)
stepfather	av χoreg	אָב חוֹרֵג (ז)
infant	tinok	תִּינוֹק (ז)
baby (infant)	tinok	תִּינוֹק (ז)
little boy, kid	pa'ot	פָּעוֹט (ז)
wife	iʃa	אִשָּׁה (נ)
husband	'ba'al	בַּעַל (ז)
spouse (husband)	ben zug	בֶּן זוּג (ז)
spouse (wife)	bat zug	בַּת זוּג (נ)
married (masc.)	nasui	נָשׂוּי
married (fem.)	nesu'a	נְשׂוּאָה
single (unmarried)	ravak	רַוָּק
bachelor	ravak	רַוָּק (ז)
divorced (masc.)	garuʃ	גָּרוּשׁ
widow	almana	אַלְמָנָה (נ)
widower	alman	אַלְמָן (ז)
relative	karov miʃpaχa	קְרוֹב מִשְׁפָּחָה (ז)
close relative	karov miʃpaχa	קְרוֹב מִשְׁפָּחָה (ז)
distant relative	karov raχok	קְרוֹב רָחוֹק (ז)
relatives	krovei miʃpaχa	קְרוֹבֵי מִשְׁפָּחָה (ז"ר)
orphan (boy)	yatom	יָתוֹם (ז)
orphan (girl)	yetoma	יְתוֹמָה (נ)
guardian (of a minor)	apo'tropos	אַפּוֹטְרוֹפּוֹס (ז)
to adopt (a boy)	le'amets	לְאַמֵּץ
to adopt (a girl)	le'amets	לְאַמֵּץ

60. Friends. Colleagues

friend (masc.)	χaver	חָבֵר (ז)
friend (fem.)	χavera	חֲבֵרָה (נ)
friendship	yedidut	יְדִידוּת (נ)
to be friends	lihyot yadidim	לִהְיוֹת יְדִידִים
pal (masc.)	χaver	חָבֵר (ז)
pal (fem.)	χavera	חֲבֵרָה (נ)

partner	ʃutaf	שׁוֹתָף (ז)
chief (boss)	menahel, roʃ	מְנַהֵל (ז), רֹאשׁ (ז)
superior (n)	memune	מְמוּנֶה (ז)
owner, proprietor	be'alim	בְּעָלִים (ז)
subordinate (n)	kafuf le	כָּפוּף ל (ז)
colleague	amit	עָמִית (ז)

acquaintance (person)	makar	מַכָּר (ז)
fellow traveller	ben levaya	בֶּן לְוָיָה (ז)
classmate	xaver lekita	חָבֵר לְכִּיתָה (ז)

neighbour (masc.)	ʃaxen	שָׁכֵן (ז)
neighbour (fem.)	ʃxena	שְׁכֵנָה (נ)
neighbours	ʃxenim	שְׁכֵנִים (ז"ר)

HUMAN BODY. MEDICINE

61. Head

head	roʃ	רֹאשׁ (ז)
face	panim	פָּנִים (ז"ר)
nose	af	אַף (ז)
mouth	pe	פֶּה (ז)
eye	'ayin	עַיִן (נ)
eyes	ei'nayim	עֵינַיִים (נ"ר)
pupil	iʃon	אִישׁוֹן (ז)
eyebrow	gaba	גַּבָּה (נ)
eyelash	ris	רִיס (ז)
eyelid	af'af	עַפְעַף (ז)
tongue	laʃon	לָשׁוֹן (נ)
tooth	ʃen	שֵׁן (נ)
lips	sfa'tayim	שְׂפָתַיִים (נ"ר)
cheekbones	atsamot leχa'yayim	עַצְמוֹת לְחָיַיִם (נ"ר)
gum	χani'χayim	חֲנִיכַיִים (ז"ר)
palate	χeχ	חֵךְ (ז)
nostrils	neχi'rayim	נְחִירַיִים (ז"ר)
chin	santer	סַנְטֵר (ז)
jaw	'leset	לֶסֶת (נ)
cheek	'leχi	לָחִי (נ)
forehead	'metsaχ	מֵצַח (ז)
temple	raka	רַקָּה (נ)
ear	'ozen	אוֹזֶן (נ)
back of the head	'oref	עוֹרֶף (ז)
neck	tsavar	צַוָּאר (ז)
throat	garon	גָּרוֹן (ז)
hair	se'ar	שֵׂיעָר (ז)
hairstyle	tis'roket	תִּסְרוֹקֶת (נ)
haircut	tis'poret	תִּסְפּוֹרֶת (נ)
wig	pe'a	פֵּאָה (נ)
moustache	safam	שָׂפָם (ז)
beard	zakan	זָקָן (ז)
to have (a beard, etc.)	legadel	לְגַדֵּל
plait	tsama	צַמָּה (נ)
sideboards	pe'ot leχa'yayim	פֵּאוֹת לְחָיַיִם (נ"ר)
red-haired (adj)	'dʒindʒi	גִ'ינגִ'י
grey (hair)	kasuf	כָּסוּף
bald (adj)	ke'reaχ	קֵירֵחַ
bald patch	ka'raχat	קָרַחַת (נ)

| ponytail | 'kuku | קוקו (ז) |
| fringe | 'poni | פוֹנִי (ז) |

62. Human body

| hand | kaf yad | כַּף יָד (נ) |
| arm | yad | יָד (נ) |

finger	'etsba	אָצְבַּע (נ)
toe	'bohen	בּוֹהֶן (נ)
thumb	agudal	אָגוּדָל (ז)
little finger	'zeret	זֶרֶת (נ)
nail	tsi'poren	צִיפּוֹרֶן (נ)

fist	egrof	אֶגְרוֹף (ז)
palm	kaf yad	כַּף יָד (נ)
wrist	ʃoreʃ kaf hayad	שוֹרֶש כַּף הַיָד (ז)
forearm	ama	אַמָה (נ)
elbow	marpek	מַרְפֵּק (ז)
shoulder	katef	כָּתֵף (נ)

leg	'regel	רֶגֶל (נ)
foot	kaf 'regel	כַּף רֶגֶל (נ)
knee	'bereχ	בֶּרֶך (נ)
calf	ʃok	שוֹק (נ)
hip	yareχ	יָרֵך (ז)
heel	akev	עָקֵב (ז)

body	guf	גוּף (ז)
stomach	'beten	בֶּטֶן (נ)
chest	χaze	חָזֶה (ז)
breast	ʃad	שַד (ז)
flank	tsad	צַד (ז)
back	gav	גַב (ז)
lower back	mot'nayim	מוֹתְנַיִים (ז"ר)
waist	'talya	טַלְיָה (נ)

navel (belly button)	tabur	טַבּוּר (ז)
buttocks	aχo'rayim	אֲחוֹרַיִים (ז"ר)
bottom	yaʃvan	יַשְבָן (ז)

beauty spot	nekudat χen	נְקוּדַת חֵן (נ)
birthmark (café au lait spot)	'ketem leida	כֶּתֶם לֵידָה (ז)
tattoo	ka'a'ku'a	קַעֲקוּעַ (ז)
scar	tsa'leket	צַלֶקֶת (נ)

63. Diseases

illness	maχala	מַחֲלָה (נ)
to be ill	lihyot χole	לִהְיוֹת חוֹלֶה
health	bri'ut	בְּרִיאוּת (נ)
runny nose (coryza)	na'zelet	נַזֶלֶת (נ)

tonsillitis	da'leket ʃkedim	דַלֶקֶת שְקֵדִים (נ)
cold (illness)	hitstanenut	הִצְטַנְנוּת (נ)
to catch a cold	lehitstanen	לְהִצְטַנֵן

bronchitis	bron'χitis	בּרוֹנכִיטִיס (ז)
pneumonia	da'leket re'ot	דַלֶקֶת רֵיאוֹת (נ)
flu, influenza	ʃa'pa'at	שַפַּעַת (נ)

shortsighted (adj)	kʦar re'iya	קְצַר רְאִיָה
longsighted (adj)	reχok re'iya	רְחוֹק־רְאִיָה
strabismus (crossed eyes)	pzila	פְּזִילָה (נ)
squint-eyed (adj)	pozel	פּוֹזֵל
cataract	katarakt	קָטָרַקט (ז)
glaucoma	gla'u'koma	גלָאוּקוֹמָה (נ)

stroke	ʃavaʦ moχi	שָבָץ מוֹחִי (ז)
heart attack	hetkef lev	הַתְקֵף לֵב (ז)
myocardial infarction	'otem ʃrir halev	אוֹטֶם שְרִיר הַלֵב (ז)
paralysis	ʃituk	שִיתוּק (ז)
to paralyse (vt)	leʃatek	לְשַתֵק

allergy	a'lergya	אָלֶרגיָה (נ)
asthma	'astma, ka'ʦeret	אַסתמָה, קַצֶרֶת (נ)
diabetes	su'keret	סוּכֶּרֶת (נ)

| toothache | ke'ev ʃi'nayim | כְּאֵב שִינַיִים (ז) |
| caries | a'ʃeʃet | עַשֶשֶת (נ) |

diarrhoea	ʃilʃul	שִלשוּל (ז)
constipation	aʦirut	עֲצִירוּת (נ)
stomach upset	kilkul keiva	קִלקוּל קֵיבָה (ז)
food poisoning	har'alat mazon	הַרעָלַת מָזוֹן (נ)
to get food poisoning	laχatof har'alat mazon	לַחֲטוֹף הַרעָלַת מָזוֹן

arthritis	da'leket mifrakim	דַלֶקֶת מִפרָקִים (נ)
rickets	ra'keχet	רַכֶּכֶת (נ)
rheumatism	ʃigaron	שִיגָרוֹן (ז)
atherosclerosis	ar'teryo skle'rosis	אַרטֶריוֹ־סקלֶרוֹסִיס (ז)

gastritis	da'leket keiva	דַלֶקֶת קֵיבָה (נ)
appendicitis	da'leket toseftan	דַלֶקֶת תוֹסֶפתָן (נ)
cholecystitis	da'leket kis hamara	דַלֶקֶת כִּיס הַמָרָה (נ)
ulcer	'ulkus, kiv	אוּלקוּס, כִּיב (ז)

measles	χa'ʦevet	חַצֶבֶת (נ)
rubella (German measles)	a'demet	אַדֶמֶת (נ)
jaundice	ʦa'hevet	צַהֶבֶת (נ)
hepatitis	da'leket kaved	דַלֶקֶת כָּבֵד (נ)

schizophrenia	sχizo'frenya	סכִיזוֹפרֶניָה (נ)
rabies (hydrophobia)	ka'levet	כַּלֶבֶת (נ)
neurosis	noi'roza	נוֹירוֹזָה (נ)
concussion	za'zu'a 'moaχ	זַעֲזוּעַ מוֹחַ (ז)

| cancer | sartan | סַרטָן (ז) |
| sclerosis | ta'reʃet | טָרֶשֶת (נ) |

multiple sclerosis	ta'reʃet nefotsa	טָרֶשֶׁת נְפוֹצָה (נ)
alcoholism	alkoholizm	אַלכּוֹהוֹלִיזם (ז)
alcoholic (n)	alkoholist	אַלכּוֹהוֹלִיסט (ז)
syphilis	a'gevet	עַגֶבֶת (נ)
AIDS	eids	אֵיידס (ז)
tumour	gidul	גִידוּל (ז)
malignant (adj)	mam'ir	מַמאִיר
benign (adj)	ʃapir	שָׁפִיר
fever	ka'daxat	קַדַחַת (נ)
malaria	ma'larya	מָלַריָה (נ)
gangrene	gan'grena	גַנגרֶנָה (נ)
seasickness	maxalat yam	מַחֲלַת יָם (נ)
epilepsy	maxalat hanefila	מַחֲלַת הַנְפִילָה (נ)
epidemic	magefa	מַגֵיפָה (נ)
typhus	'tifus	טִיפוּס (ז)
tuberculosis	ʃa'xefet	שַׁחֶפֶת (נ)
cholera	ko'lera	כּוֹלֵרָה (נ)
plague (bubonic ~)	davar	דֶבֶר (ז)

64. Symptoms. Treatments. Part 1

symptom	simptom	סִימפּטוֹם (ז)
temperature	xom	חוֹם (ז)
high temperature (fever)	xom ga'voha	חוֹם גָבוֹהַ (ז)
pulse (heartbeat)	'dofek	דוֹפֶק (ז)
dizziness (vertigo)	sxar'xoret	סחַרחוֹרֶת (נ)
hot (adj)	xam	חַם
shivering	tsmar'moret	צמַרמוֹרֶת (נ)
pale (e.g. ~ face)	xiver	חִיוֵור
cough	ʃi'ul	שִׁיעוּל (ז)
to cough (vi)	lehiʃta‘el	לְהִשׁתַעֵל
to sneeze (vi)	lehit‘ateʃ	לְהִתעַטֵשׁ
faint	ilafon	עִילָפוֹן (ז)
to faint (vi)	lehit‘alef	לְהִתעַלֵף
bruise (hématome)	xabura	חַבּוּרָה (נ)
bump (lump)	blita	בּלִיטָה (נ)
to bang (bump)	lekabel maka	לְקַבֵּל מַכָּה
contusion (bruise)	maka	מַכָּה (נ)
to get a bruise	lekabel maka	לְקַבֵּל מַכָּה
to limp (vi)	lits'lo‘a	לִצלוֹעַ
dislocation	'neka	נֶקַע (ז)
to dislocate (vt)	lin'ko‘a	לִנקוֹעַ
fracture	'ʃever	שֶׁבֶר (ז)
to have a fracture	liʃbor	לִשׁבּוֹר
cut (e.g. paper ~)	xatax	חָתָך (ז)
to cut oneself	lehixatex	לְהֵיחָתֵך

bleeding	dimum	דִימוּם (ז)
burn (injury)	kviya	כְּוְוָיָה (נ)
to get burned	laxatof kviya	לַחֲטוֹף כְּוְוָיָה
to prick (vt)	lidkor	לִדְקוֹר
to prick oneself	lehidaker	לְהִידָקֵר
to injure (vt)	liftso'a	לִפְצוֹעַ
injury	ptsi'a	פְּצִיעָה (נ)
wound	'petsa	פֶּצַע (ז)
trauma	'tra'uma	טְרָאוּמָה (נ)
to be delirious	lahazot	לַהֲזוֹת
to stutter (vi)	legamgem	לְגַמְגֵם
sunstroke	makat 'ʃemeʃ	מַכַּת שֶׁמֶשׁ (נ)

65. Symptoms. Treatments. Part 2

pain, ache	ke'ev	כְּאֵב (ז)
splinter (in foot, etc.)	kots	קוֹץ (ז)
sweat (perspiration)	ze'a	זֵיעָה (נ)
to sweat (perspire)	leha'zi'a	לְהַזִיעַ
vomiting	haka'a	הֲקָאָה (נ)
convulsions	pirkusim	פִּירְפּוּסִים (ז"ר)
pregnant (adj)	hara	הָרָה
to be born	lehivaled	לְהִיוָולֵד
delivery, labour	leda	לֵידָה (נ)
to deliver (~ a baby)	la'ledet	לָלֶדֶת
abortion	hapala	הַפָּלָה (נ)
breathing, respiration	neʃima	נְשִׁימָה (נ)
in-breath (inhalation)	ʃe'ifa	שְׁאִיפָה (נ)
out-breath (exhalation)	neʃifa	נְשִׁיפָה (נ)
to exhale (breathe out)	linʃof	לִנְשׁוֹף
to inhale (vi)	liʃ'of	לִשְׁאוֹף
disabled person	naxe	נָכֶה (ז)
cripple	naxe	נָכֶה (ז)
drug addict	narkoman	נַרְקוֹמָן (ז)
deaf (adj)	xereʃ	חֵירֵשׁ
mute (adj)	ilem	אִילֵם
deaf mute (adj)	xereʃ-ilem	חֵירֵשׁ-אִילֵם
mad, insane (adj)	meʃuga	מְשׁוּגָע
madman (demented person)	meʃuga	מְשׁוּגָע (ז)
madwoman	meʃu'ga'at	מְשׁוּגַעַת (נ)
to go insane	lehiʃta'ge'a	לְהִשְׁתַגֵעַ
gene	gen	גֵן (ז)
immunity	xasinut	חֲסִינוּת (נ)
hereditary (adj)	toraʃti	תּוֹרַשְׁתִי

congenital (adj)	mulad	מוּלָד
virus	'virus	וִירוּס (ז)
microbe	xaidak	חַיְדָּק (ז)
bacterium	bak'terya	בַּקְטֶרְיָה (נ)
infection	zihum	זִיהוּם (ז)

66. Symptoms. Treatments. Part 3

hospital	beit xolim	בֵּית חוֹלִים (ז)
patient	metupal	מְטוּפָּל (ז)
diagnosis	avxana	אַבחָנָה (נ)
cure	ripui	רִיפּוּי (ז)
medical treatment	tipul refu'i	טִיפּוּל רְפוּאִי (ז)
to get treatment	lekabel tipul	לְקַבֵּל טִיפּוּל
to treat (~ a patient)	letapel be...	לְטַפֵּל בְּ...
to nurse (look after)	letapel be...	לְטַפֵּל בְּ...
care (nursing ~)	tipul	טִיפּוּל (ז)
operation, surgery	ni'tuax	נִיתוּח (ז)
to bandage (head, limb)	laxbo∫	לַחבּוֹש
bandaging	xavi∫a	חֲבִישָה (נ)
vaccination	xisun	חִיסוּן (ז)
to vaccinate (vt)	lexasen	לְחַסֵן
injection	zrika	זְרִיקָה (נ)
to give an injection	lehazrik	לְהַזְרִיק
attack	hetkef	הֶתקֵף (ז)
amputation	kti'a	קְטִיעָה (נ)
to amputate (vt)	lik'to'a	לִקטוֹעַ
coma	tar'demet	תַרדֶמֶת (נ)
to be in a coma	lihyot betar'demet	לִהיוֹת בְּתַרדֶמֶת
intensive care	tipul nimra∫	טִיפּוּל נִמרָץ (ז)
to recover (~ from flu)	lehaxlim	לְהַחלִים
condition (patient's ~)	ma∫sav	מַצָּב (ז)
consciousness	hakara	הַכָּרָה (נ)
memory (faculty)	zikaron	זִיכָּרוֹן (ז)
to pull out (tooth)	la'akor	לַעֲקוֹר
filling	stima	סְתִימָה (נ)
to fill (a tooth)	la'asot stima	לַעֲשוֹת סְתִימָה
hypnosis	hip'noza	הִיפּנוֹזָה (נ)
to hypnotize (vt)	lehapnet	לְהַפנֵט

67. Medicine. Drugs. Accessories

medicine, drug	trufa	תְרוּפָה (נ)
remedy	trufa	תְרוּפָה (נ)
to prescribe (vt)	lir∫om	לִרשוֹם

prescription	mirʃam	מִרְשָׁם (ז)
tablet, pill	kadur	כַּדּוּר (ז)
ointment	miʃχa	מִשְׁחָה (נ)
ampoule	'ampula	אַמְפּוּלָה (נ)
mixture, solution	ta'a'rovet	תַּעֲרוֹבֶת (נ)
syrup	sirop	סִירוֹף (ז)
capsule	gluya	גְּלוּיָה (נ)
powder	avka	אַבְקָה (נ)

gauze bandage	taχ'boʃet 'gaza	תַּחְבּוֹשֶׁת גָּאזָה (נ)
cotton wool	'ʦemer 'gefen	צֶמֶר גֶּפֶן (ז)
iodine	yod	יוֹד (ז)

plaster	'plaster	פְּלַסְטֶר (ז)
eyedropper	taf'tefet	טַפְטֶפֶת (נ)
thermometer	madχom	מַדְחוֹם (ז)
syringe	mazrek	מַזְרֵק (ז)

| wheelchair | kise galgalim | כִּיסֵא גַּלְגַּלִים (ז) |
| crutches | ka'bayim | קַבַּיִים (ז"ר) |

painkiller	meʃakeχ ke'evim	מְשַׁכֵּךְ כְּאֵבִים (ז)
laxative	trufa meʃal'ʃelet	תְּרוּפָה מְשַׁלְשֶׁלֶת (נ)
spirits (ethanol)	'kohal	כּוֹהַל (ז)
medicinal herbs	isvei marpe	עִשְׂבֵי מַרְפֵּא (ז"ר)
herbal (~ tea)	ʃel asavim	שֶׁל עֲשָׂבִים

FLAT

68. Flat

flat	dira	דִּירָה (נ)
room	'xeder	חֶדֶר (ז)
bedroom	xadar ʃena	חֲדַר שֵׁינָה (ז)
dining room	pinat 'oxel	פִּינַת אוֹכֶל (נ)
living room	salon	סָלוֹן (ז)
study (home office)	xadar avoda	חֲדַר עֲבוֹדָה (ז)
entry room	prozdor	פְּרוֹזדוֹר (ז)
bathroom	xadar am'batya	חֲדַר אַמבַּטיָה (ז)
water closet	ʃerutim	שֵׁירוּתִים (ז"ר)
ceiling	tikra	תִּקרָה (נ)
floor	ritspa	רִצפָּה (נ)
corner	pina	פִּינָה (נ)

69. Furniture. Interior

furniture	rehitim	רָהִיטִים (ז"ר)
table	ʃulxan	שׁוּלחָן (ז)
chair	kise	כִּסֵא (ז)
bed	mita	מִיטָה (נ)
sofa, settee	sapa	סַפָּה (נ)
armchair	kursa	כּוּרסָה (נ)
bookcase	aron sfarim	אֲרוֹן סְפָרִים (ז)
shelf	madaf	מַדָּף (ז)
wardrobe	aron bgadim	אֲרוֹן בְּגָדִים (ז)
coat rack (wall-mounted ~)	mitle	מִתלֶה (ז)
coat stand	mitle	מִתלֶה (ז)
chest of drawers	ʃida	שִׁידָה (נ)
coffee table	ʃulxan itonim	שׁוּלחַן עִיתוֹנִים (ז)
mirror	mar'a	מַראָה (נ)
carpet	ʃa'tiax	שָׁטִיחַ (ז)
small carpet	ʃa'tiax	שָׁטִיחַ (ז)
fireplace	ax	אָח (נ)
candle	ner	נֵר (ז)
candlestick	pamot	פָּמוֹט (ז)
drapes	vilonot	וִילוֹנוֹת (ז"ר)
wallpaper	tapet	טַפֵּט (ז)

blinds (jalousie)	trisim	תְּרִיסִים (ז״ר)
table lamp	menorat ʃulxan	מְנוֹרַת שׁוּלחָן (נ)
wall lamp (sconce)	menorat kir	מְנוֹרַת קִיר (נ)
standard lamp	menora o'medet	מְנוֹרָה עוֹמֶדֶת (נ)
chandelier	niv'reʃet	נִברֶשֶׁת (נ)
leg (of a chair, table)	'regel	רֶגֶל (נ)
armrest	miʃ'enet yad	מִשׁעֶנֶת יָד (נ)
back (backrest)	miʃ'enet	מִשׁעֶנֶת (נ)
drawer	megera	מְגֵירָה (נ)

70. Bedding

bedclothes	matsa'im	מַצָעִים (ז״ר)
pillow	karit	כָּרִית (נ)
pillowslip	tsipit	צִיפִית (נ)
duvet	smixa	שׂמִיכָה (נ)
sheet	sadin	סָדִין (ז)
bedspread	kisui mita	כִּיסוּי מִיטָה (ז)

71. Kitchen

kitchen	mitbax	מִטבָּח (ז)
gas	gaz	גָז (ז)
gas cooker	tanur gaz	תַנוּר גָז (ז)
electric cooker	tanur xaʃmali	תַנוּר חַשׁמַלִי (ז)
oven	tanur afiya	תַנוּר אֲפִיָה (ז)
microwave oven	mikrogal	מִיקרוֹגַל (ז)
refrigerator	mekarer	מְקָרֵר (ז)
freezer	makpi	מַקפִּיא (ז)
dishwasher	me'diax kelim	מֵדִיחַ כֵּלִים (ז)
mincer	matxenat basar	מַטחֵנַת בָּשָׂר (נ)
juicer	masxeta	מַסחֵטָה (נ)
toaster	'toster	טוֹסטֶר (ז)
mixer	'mikser	מִיקסֶר (ז)
coffee machine	mexonat kafe	מְכוֹנַת קָפֶה (נ)
coffee pot	findʒan	פִינג'אן (ז)
coffee grinder	matxenat kafe	מַטחֵנַת קָפֶה (נ)
kettle	kumkum	קוּמקוּם (ז)
teapot	kumkum	קוּמקוּם (ז)
lid	mixse	מִכסֶה (ז)
tea strainer	mis'nenet te	מְסַנֶנֶת תֶה (נ)
spoon	kaf	כַּף (נ)
teaspoon	kapit	כַּפִּית (נ)
soup spoon	kaf	כַּף (נ)
fork	mazleg	מַזלֵג (ז)
knife	sakin	סַכִּין (ז, נ)

tableware (dishes)	kelim	כֵּלִים (ז״ר)
plate (dinner ~)	tsa'laxat	צַלַּחַת (נ)
saucer	taxtit	תַּחְתִּית (נ)
shot glass	kosit	כּוֹסִית (נ)
glass (tumbler)	kos	כּוֹס (נ)
cup	'sefel	סֵפֶל (ז)
sugar bowl	mis'keret	מִסְכֶּרֶת (נ)
salt cellar	milxiya	מִלְחִיָּה (נ)
pepper pot	pilpeliya	פִּלְפְּלִיָּה (נ)
butter dish	maxame'a	מַחְמֵאָה (נ)
stock pot (soup pot)	sir	סִיר (ז)
frying pan (skillet)	maxvat	מַחֲבַת (נ)
ladle	tarvad	תַּרְוָד (ז)
colander	mis'nenet	מְסַנֶּנֶת (נ)
tray (serving ~)	magaʃ	מַגָּשׁ (ז)
bottle	bakbuk	בַּקְבּוּק (ז)
jar (glass)	tsin'tsenet	צִנְצֶנֶת (נ)
tin (can)	paxit	פַּחִית (נ)
bottle opener	potxan bakbukim	פּוֹתְחָן בַּקְבּוּקִים (ז)
tin opener	potxan kufsa'ot	פּוֹתְחָן קוּפְסָאוֹת (ז)
corkscrew	maxlets	מַחְלֵץ (ז)
filter	'filter	פִילְטֶר (ז)
to filter (vt)	lesanen	לְסַנֵּן
waste (food ~, etc.)	'zevel	זֶבֶל (ז)
waste bin (kitchen ~)	pax 'zevel	פַּח זֶבֶל (ז)

72. Bathroom

bathroom	xadar am'batya	חֲדַר אַמְבַּטְיָה (ז)
water	'mayim	מַיִם (ז״ר)
tap	'berez	בֶּרֶז (ז)
hot water	'mayim xamim	מַיִם חַמִּים (ז״ר)
cold water	'mayim karim	מַיִם קָרִים (ז״ר)
toothpaste	miʃxat ʃi'nayim	מִשְׁחַת שִׁנַּיִים (נ)
to clean one's teeth	letsax'tseax ʃi'nayim	לְצַחְצֵחַ שִׁנַּיִים
toothbrush	miv'reʃet ʃi'nayim	מִבְרֶשֶׁת שִׁנַּיִים (נ)
to shave (vi)	lehitga'leax	לְהִתְגַּלֵּחַ
shaving foam	'ketsef gi'luax	קֶצֶף גִּילּוּחַ (ז)
razor	'ta'ar	תַּעַר (ז)
to wash (one's hands, etc.)	liʃtof	לִשְׁטוֹף
to have a bath	lehitraxets	לְהִתְרַחֵץ
shower	mik'laxat	מִקְלַחַת (נ)
to have a shower	lehitka'leax	לְהִתְקַלֵּחַ
bath	am'batya	אַמְבַּטְיָה (נ)
toilet (toilet bowl)	asla	אַסְלָה (נ)

sink (washbasin)	kiyor	כִּיּוֹר (ז)
soap	sabon	סַבּוֹן (ז)
soap dish	saboniya	סַבּוֹנִיָּה (נ)
sponge	sfog 'lifa	סְפוֹג לִיפָה (ז)
shampoo	ʃampu	שַׁמְפּוּ (ז)
towel	ma'gevet	מַגֶּבֶת (נ)
bathrobe	χaluk raχatsa	חָלוּק רַחְצָה (ז)
laundry (laundering)	kvisa	כְּבִיסָה (נ)
washing machine	meχonat kvisa	מְכוֹנַת כְּבִיסָה (נ)
to do the laundry	leχabes	לְכַבֵּס
washing powder	avkat kvisa	אַבְקַת כְּבִיסָה (נ)

73. Household appliances

TV, telly	tele'vizya	טֶלֶוִויזְיָה (נ)
tape recorder	teip	טֵייפ (ז)
video	maχʃir 'vide'o	מַכְשִׁיר וִידֵאוֹ (ז)
radio	'radyo	רַדְיוֹ (ז)
player (CD, MP3, etc.)	nagan	נַגָּן (ז)
video projector	makren	מַקְרֵן (ז)
home cinema	kol'no'a beiti	קוֹלְנוֹעַ בֵּיתִי (ז)
DVD player	nagan dividi	נַגָּן DVD (ז)
amplifier	magber	מַגְבֵּר (ז)
video game console	maχʃir plei'steiʃen	מַכְשִׁיר פְּלֵייסְטֵיישֶׁן (ז)
video camera	matslemat 'vide'o	מַצְלֵמַת וִידֵאוֹ (נ)
camera (photo)	matslema	מַצְלֵמָה (נ)
digital camera	matslema digi'talit	מַצְלֵמָה דִּיגִיטָלִית (נ)
vacuum cleaner	ʃo'ev avak	שׁוֹאֵב אָבָק (ז)
iron (e.g. steam ~)	maghets	מַגְהֵץ (ז)
ironing board	'kereʃ gihuts	קֶרֶשׁ גִּיהוּץ (ז)
telephone	'telefon	טֶלֶפוֹן (ז)
mobile phone	'telefon nayad	טֶלֶפוֹן נַיָּיד (ז)
typewriter	meχonat ktiva	מְכוֹנַת כְּתִיבָה (נ)
sewing machine	meχonat tfira	מְכוֹנַת תְּפִירָה (נ)
microphone	mikrofon	מִיקְרוֹפוֹן (ז)
headphones	ozniyot	אוֹזְנִיּוֹת (נ"ר)
remote control (TV)	'ʃelet	שֶׁלֶט (ז)
CD, compact disc	taklitor	תַּקְלִיטוֹר (ז)
cassette, tape	ka'letet	קַלֶּטֶת (נ)
vinyl record	taklit	תַּקְלִיט (ז)

THE EARTH. WEATHER

74. Outer space

space	χalal	חָלָל (ז)
space (as adj)	ʃel χalal	שֶׁל חָלָל
outer space	χalal χitson	חָלָל חִיצוֹן (ז)
world	olam	עוֹלָם (ז)
universe	yekum	יְקוּם (ז)
galaxy	ga'laksya	גָּלַקְסִיָה (נ)
star	koχav	כּוֹכָב (ז)
constellation	tsvir koχavim	צְבִיר כּוֹכָבִים (ז)
planet	koχav 'leχet	כּוֹכָב לֶכֶת (ז)
satellite	lavyan	לַוְיָן (ז)
meteorite	mete'orit	מֶטֶאוֹרִיט (ז)
comet	koχav ʃavit	כּוֹכָב שָׁבִיט (ז)
asteroid	aste'ro'id	אַסְטֶרוֹאִיד (ז)
orbit	maslul	מַסְלוּל (ז)
to revolve	lesovev	לְסוֹבֵב
(~ around the Earth)		
atmosphere	atmos'fera	אַטְמוֹסְפֵרָה (נ)
the Sun	'ʃemeʃ	שֶׁמֶשׁ (נ)
solar system	ma'a'reχet ha'ʃemeʃ	מַעֲרֶכֶת הַשֶּׁמֶשׁ (נ)
solar eclipse	likui χama	לִיקוּי חַמָה (ז)
the Earth	kadur ha''arets	כַּדוּר הָאָרֶץ (ז)
the Moon	ya'reaχ	יָרֵחַ (ז)
Mars	ma'adim	מַאֲדִים (ז)
Venus	'noga	נוֹגַּה (ז)
Jupiter	'tsedek	צֶדֶק (ז)
Saturn	ʃabtai	שַׁבְּתַאי (ז)
Mercury	koχav χama	כּוֹכָב חַמָה (ז)
Uranus	u'ranus	אוּרָנוּס (ז)
Neptune	neptun	נֶפְטוּן (ז)
Pluto	'pluto	פְּלוּטוֹ (ז)
Milky Way	ʃvil haχalav	שְׁבִיל הֶחָלָב (ז)
Great Bear (Ursa Major)	duba gdola	דוּבָּה גְדוֹלָה (נ)
North Star	koχav hatsafon	כּוֹכָב הַצָפוֹן (ז)
Martian	toʃav ma'adim	תּוֹשַׁב מַאֲדִים (ז)
extraterrestrial (n)	χutsan	חוּצָן (ז)
alien	χaizar	חַייָזָר (ז)

flying saucer	tsa'laxat me'o'fefet	צַלַחַת מְעוֹפֶפֶת (נ)
spaceship	xalalit	חֲלָלִית (נ)
space station	taxanat xalal	תַחֲנַת חָלָל (נ)
blast-off	hamra'a	הַמְרָאָה (נ)
engine	ma'no'a	מָנוֹעַ (ז)
nozzle	nexir	נְחִיר (ז)
fuel	'delek	דֶלֶק (ז)
cockpit, flight deck	'kokpit	קוֹקְפִּיט (ז)
aerial	an'tena	אַנטֶנָה (נ)
porthole	eʃnav	אֶשׁנָב (ז)
solar panel	'luax so'lari	לוּחַ סוֹלָרִי (ז)
spacesuit	xalifat xalal	חֲלִיפַת חָלָל (נ)
weightlessness	'xoser miʃkal	חוֹסֶר מִשׁקָל (ז)
oxygen	xamtsan	חַמצָן (ז)
docking (in space)	agina	עֲגִינָה (נ)
to dock (vi, vt)	la'agon	לַעֲגוֹן
observatory	mitspe koxavim	מִצפֶּה כּוֹכָבִים (ז)
telescope	teleskop	טֶלֶסקוֹפּ (ז)
to observe (vt)	liʦpot, lehaʃkif	לצפות, להשקיף
to explore (vt)	laxkor	לַחקוֹר

75. The Earth

the Earth	kadur ha''arets	כַּדוּר הָאָרֶץ (ז)
the globe (the Earth)	kadur ha''arets	כַּדוּר הָאָרֶץ (ז)
planet	koxav 'lexet	כּוֹכַב לֶכֶת (ז)
atmosphere	atmos'fera	אַטמוֹספֶרָה (נ)
geography	ge'o'grafya	גִיאוֹגרַפיָה (נ)
nature	'teva	טֶבַע (ז)
globe (table ~)	'globus	גלוֹבּוּס (ז)
map	mapa	מַפָּה (נ)
atlas	'atlas	אַטלָס (ז)
Europe	ei'ropa	אֵירוֹפָּה (נ)
Asia	'asya	אַסיָה (נ)
Africa	'afrika	אַפרִיקָה (נ)
Australia	ost'ralya	אוֹסטרַליָה (נ)
America	a'merika	אָמֶרִיקָה (נ)
North America	a'merika hatsfonit	אָמֶרִיקָה הַצפוֹנִית (נ)
South America	a'merika hadromit	אָמֶרִיקָה הַדרוֹמִית (נ)
Antarctica	ya'beʃet an'tarktika	יַבֶּשֶׁת אַנטַארקטִיקָה (נ)
the Arctic	'arktika	אַרקטִיקָה (נ)

76. Cardinal directions

north	tsafon	צָפוֹן (ז)
to the north	tsa'fona	צָפוֹנָה
in the north	batsafon	בַּצָּפוֹן
northern (adj)	tsfoni	צפוֹנִי

south	darom	דָרוֹם (ז)
to the south	da'roma	דָרוֹמָה
in the south	badarom	בַּדָרוֹם
southern (adj)	dromi	דרוֹמִי

west	maʿarav	מַעֲרָב (ז)
to the west	maʿaʿrava	מַעֲרָבָה
in the west	bamaʿarav	בַּמַעֲרָב
western (adj)	maʿaravi	מַעֲרָבִי

east	mizraχ	מִזרָח (ז)
to the east	miz'raχa	מִזרָחָה
in the east	bamizraχ	בַּמִזרָח
eastern (adj)	mizraχi	מִזרָחִי

77. Sea. Ocean

sea	yam	יָם (ז)
ocean	ok'yanos	אוֹקיָאנוֹס (ז)
gulf (bay)	mifrats	מִפרָץ (ז)
straits	meitsar	מֵיצָר (ז)

land (solid ground)	yabaʃa	יַבָּשָׁה (נ)
continent (mainland)	ya'beʃet	יַבֶּשֶׁת (נ)
island	i	אִי (ז)
peninsula	χatsi i	חֲצִי אִי (ז)
archipelago	arχipelag	אַרכִיפֶּלָג (ז)

bay, cove	mifrats	מִפרָץ (ז)
harbour	namal	נָמָל (ז)
lagoon	la'guna	לָגוּנָה (נ)
cape	kef	כֵּף (ז)

atoll	atol	אָטוֹל (ז)
reef	ʃunit	שׁוֹנִית (נ)
coral	almog	אַלמוֹג (ז)
coral reef	ʃunit almogim	שׁוֹנִית אַלמוֹגִים (נ)

deep (adj)	amok	עָמוֹק
depth (deep water)	'omek	עוֹמֶק (ז)
abyss	tehom	תְהוֹם (נ)
trench (e.g. Mariana ~)	maχteʃ	מַכתֵּשׁ (ז)

current (Ocean ~)	'zerem	זֶרֶם (ז)
to surround (bathe)	lehakif	לְהַקִיף
shore	χof	חוֹף (ז)

coast	χof yam	חוֹף יָם (ז)
flow (flood tide)	ge'ut	גָּאוּת (נ)
ebb (ebb tide)	'ʃefel	שֶׁפֶל (ז)
shoal	sirton	שִׂרטוֹן (ז)
bottom (~ of the sea)	karka'it	קַרקָעִית (נ)
wave	gal	גַּל (ז)
crest (~ of a wave)	pisgat hagal	פְּסגַת הַגַּל (נ)
spume (sea foam)	'ketsef	קֶצֶף (ז)
storm (sea storm)	sufa	סוּפָה (נ)
hurricane	hurikan	הוֹרִיקָן (ז)
tsunami	tsu'nami	צוּנָאמִי (ז)
calm (dead ~)	'roga	רוֹגַע (ז)
quiet, calm (adj)	ʃalev	שָׁלֵו
pole	'kotev	קוֹטֶב (ז)
polar (adj)	kotbi	קוֹטבִּי
latitude	kav 'roχav	קו רוֹחַב (ז)
longitude	kav 'oreχ	קו אוֹרֶך (ז)
parallel	kav 'roχav	קו רוֹחַב (ז)
equator	kav hamaʃve	קו הַמַשׁוֶוה (ז)
sky	ʃa'mayim	שָׁמַיִם (ז"ר)
horizon	'ofek	אוֹפֶק (ז)
air	avir	אֲוֹויר (ז)
lighthouse	migdalor	מִגדָלוֹר (ז)
to dive (vi)	litslol	לִצלוֹל
to sink (ab. boat)	lit'bo'a	לִטבּוֹעַ
treasure	otsarot	אוֹצָרוֹת (ז"ר)

78. Seas & Oceans names

Atlantic Ocean	ha'ok'yanus ha'at'lanti	הָאוֹקיָינוֹס הָאַטלַנטִי (ז)
Indian Ocean	ha'ok'yanus ha'hodi	הָאוֹקיָינוֹס הַהוֹדִי (ז)
Pacific Ocean	ha'ok'yanus haʃaket	הָאוֹקיָינוֹס הַשֶׁקֶט (ז)
Arctic Ocean	ok'yanos ha'keraχ hatsfoni	אוֹקיָינוֹס הַקֶרַח הַצפוֹנִי (ז)
Black Sea	hayam haʃaχor	הַיָם הַשָׁחוֹר (ז)
Red Sea	yam suf	יַם סוּף (ז)
Yellow Sea	hayam hatsahov	הַיָם הַצָהוֹב (ז)
White Sea	hayam halavan	הַיָם הַלָבָן (ז)
Caspian Sea	hayam ha'kaspi	הַיָם הַכַּספִּי (ז)
Dead Sea	yam ha'melaχ	יַם הַמֶלַח (ז)
Mediterranean Sea	hayam hatiχon	הַיָם הַתִיכוֹן (ז)
Aegean Sea	hayam ha'e'ge'i	הַיָם הָאֶגֶאִי (ז)
Adriatic Sea	hayam ha'adri'yati	הַיָם הָאַדרִיָיאתִי (ז)
Arabian Sea	hayam ha'aravi	הַיָם הָעֲרָבִי (ז)
Sea of Japan	hayam haya'pani	הַיָם הַיָפָנִי (ז)

Bering Sea	yam 'bering	יַם בֶּרִינג (ז)
South China Sea	yam sin hadromi	יַם סִין הַדרוֹמִי (ז)
Coral Sea	yam ha'almogim	יַם הָאַלמוֹגִים (ז)
Tasman Sea	yam tasman	יַם טַסמַן (ז)
Caribbean Sea	hayam haka'ribi	הַיָם הַקָרִיבִּי (ז)
Barents Sea	yam 'barents	יַם בָּרֶנץ (ז)
Kara Sea	yam 'kara	יַם קָארָה (ז)
North Sea	hayam hatsfoni	הַיָם הַצפוֹנִי (ז)
Baltic Sea	hayam ha'balti	הַיָם הַבַּלטִי (ז)
Norwegian Sea	hayam hanor'vegi	הַיָם הַנוֹרבֶּגִי (ז)

79. Mountains

mountain	har	הַר (ז)
mountain range	'reχes harim	רֶכֶס הָרִים (ז)
mountain ridge	'reχes har	רֶכֶס הַר (ז)
summit, top	pisga	פִּסגָה (נ)
peak	pisga	פִּסגָה (נ)
foot (~ of the mountain)	margelot	מַרגְלוֹת (נ"ר)
slope (mountainside)	midron	מִדרוֹן (ז)
volcano	har 'ga'aʃ	הַר גַעַש (ז)
active volcano	har 'ga'aʃ pa'il	הַר גַעַש פָּעִיל (ז)
dormant volcano	har 'ga'aʃ radum	הַר גַעַש רָדוּם (ז)
eruption	hitpartsut	הִתפָּרצוּת (נ)
crater	lo'a	לוֹעַ (ז)
magma	megama	מַגמָה (נ)
lava	'lava	לָאבָה (נ)
molten (~ lava)	lohet	לוֹהֵט
canyon	kanyon	קַניוֹן (ז)
gorge	gai	גַיא (ז)
crevice	'beka	בֶּקַע (ז)
abyss (chasm)	tehom	תְהוֹם (נ)
pass, col	ma'avar harim	מַעֲבַר הָרִים (ז)
plateau	rama	רָמָה (נ)
cliff	tsuk	צוּק (ז)
hill	giv'a	גִבעָה (נ)
glacier	karχon	קַרחוֹן (ז)
waterfall	mapal 'mayim	מַפַּל מַיִם (ז)
geyser	'geizer	גֵייזֶר (ז)
lake	agam	אֲגַם (ז)
plain	miʃor	מִישוֹר (ז)
landscape	nof	נוֹף (ז)
echo	hed	הֵד (ז)
alpinist	metapes harim	מְטַפֵּס הָרִים (ז)

rock climber	metapes sla'im	מְטַפֵּס סְלָעִים (ז)
to conquer (in climbing)	liχboʃ	לִכְבּוֹש
climb (an easy ~)	tipus	טִיפּוּס (ז)

80. Mountains names

The Alps	harei ha"alpim	הָרֵי הָאַלְפִּים (ז"ר)
Mont Blanc	mon blan	מוֹן בְּלָאן (ז)
The Pyrenees	pire'ne'im	פִּירֶנָאִים (ז"ר)

The Carpathians	kar'patim	קַרְפָּטִים (ז"ר)
The Ural Mountains	harei ural	הָרֵי אוּרָל (ז"ר)
The Caucasus Mountains	harei hakavkaz	הָרֵי הַקַוְוקָז (ז"ר)
Mount Elbrus	elbrus	אֶלְבְּרוּס (ז)

The Altai Mountains	harei altai	הָרֵי אַלְטַאי (ז"ר)
The Tian Shan	tyan ʃan	טְיָאן שָאן (ז)
The Pamirs	harei pamir	הָרֵי פָּאמִיר (ז"ר)
The Himalayas	harei hehima'laya	הָרֵי הַהִימָלָאיָה (ז"ר)
Mount Everest	everest	אֶוֶורֶסְט (ז)

| The Andes | harei ha"andim | הָרֵי הָאַנְדִים (ז"ר) |
| Mount Kilimanjaro | kiliman'dʒaro | קִילִימַנְגָ'רוֹ (ז) |

81. Rivers

river	nahar	נָהָר (ז)
spring (natural source)	ma'ayan	מַעְיָין (ז)
riverbed (river channel)	afik	אָפִיק (ז)
basin (river valley)	agan nahar	אֲגַן נָהָר (ז)
to flow into ...	lehiʃapeχ	לְהִישָפֵּך

| tributary | yuval | יוּבָל (ז) |
| bank (river ~) | χof | חוֹף (ז) |

current (stream)	'zerem	זֶרֶם (ז)
downstream (adv)	bemorad hanahar	בְּמוֹרַד הַנָהָר
upstream (adv)	bema'ale hanahar	בְּמַעֲלֵה הַזֶרֶם

inundation	hatsafa	הֲצָפָה (נ)
flooding	ʃitafon	שִיטָפוֹן (ז)
to overflow (vi)	la'alot al gdotav	לַעֲלוֹת עַל גְדוֹתָיו
to flood (vt)	lehatsif	לְהָצִיף

| shallow (shoal) | sirton | שִׂרְטוֹן (ז) |
| rapids | 'eʃed | אָשֶד (ז) |

dam	'seχer	סֶכֶר (ז)
canal	te'ala	תְעָלָה (נ)
reservoir (artificial lake)	ma'agar 'mayim	מַאֲגַר מַיִם (ז)
sluice, lock	ta 'ʃayit	תָא שַיִט (ז)
water body (pond, etc.)	ma'agar 'mayim	מַאֲגַר מַיִם (ז)

swamp (marshland)	biţsa	בִּיצָה (נ)
bog, marsh	biţsa	בִּיצָה (נ)
whirlpool	me'ar'bolet	מְעַרְבֹּלֶת (נ)

stream (brook)	'naχal	נַחַל (ז)
drinking (ab. water)	ʃel ʃtiya	שֶׁל שתִיָיה
fresh (~ water)	metukim	מְתוּקִים

| ice | 'keraχ | קֶרַח (ז) |
| to freeze over (ab. river, etc.) | likpo | לִקפֹּוא |

82. Rivers names

| Seine | hasen | הַסֵן (ז) |
| Loire | lu'ar | לוּאָר (ז) |

Thames	'temza	תֶמזָה (ז)
Rhine	hrain	הַרַיין (ז)
Danube	da'nuba	דָנוּבָה (ז)

Volga	'volga	וֹולגָה (ז)
Don	nahar don	נָהָר דוֹן (ז)
Lena	'lena	לֶנָה (ז)

Yellow River	hvang ho	הוַונג הוֹ (ז)
Yangtze	yangţse	יַאנגצֶה (ז)
Mekong	mekong	מֶקוֹנג (ז)
Ganges	'ganges	גַנגֶס (ז)

Nile River	'nilus	נִילוּס (ז)
Congo River	'kongo	קוֹנגוֹ (ז)
Okavango River	ok'vango	אוֹקָבַנגוֹ (ז)
Zambezi River	zam'bezi	זַמבֶּזִי (ז)
Limpopo River	limpopo	לִימפוֹפוֹ (ז)
Mississippi River	misi'sipi	מִיסִיסִיפִּי (ז)

83. Forest

| forest, wood | 'ya'ar | יַעַר (ז) |
| forest (as adj) | ʃel 'ya'ar | שֶׁל יַעַר |

thick forest	avi ha'ya'ar	עֲבִי הַיַעַר (ז)
grove	χurʃa	חוֹרשָׁה (נ)
forest clearing	ka'raχat 'ya'ar	קָרַחַת יַעַר (נ)

| thicket | svaχ | סְבָךְ (ז) |
| scrubland | 'siaχ | שִׂיחַ (ז) |

footpath (troddenpath)	ʃvil	שׁבִיל (ז)
gully	'emek ţsar	עֵמֶק צַר (ז)
tree	eţs	עֵץ (ז)
leaf	ale	עָלֶה (ז)

leaves (foliage)	alva	עָלְוָה (נ)
fall of leaves	ʃa'leχet	שַׁלֶּכֶת (נ)
to fall (ab. leaves)	linʃor	לִנְשׁוֹר
top (of the tree)	tsa'meret	צַמֶּרֶת (נ)
branch	anaf	עָנָף (ז)
bough	anaf ave	עָנָף עָבֶה (ז)
bud (on shrub, tree)	nitsan	נִיצָן (ז)
needle (of the pine tree)	'maχat	מַחַט (נ)
fir cone	itstrubal	אָצְטְרוּבָּל (ז)
tree hollow	χor ba'ets	חוֹר בָּעֵץ (ז)
nest	ken	קֵן (ז)
burrow (animal hole)	meχila	מְחִילָה (נ)
trunk	'geza	גֶּזַע (ז)
root	'ʃoreʃ	שׁוֹרֶשׁ (ז)
bark	klipa	קְלִיפָּה (נ)
moss	taχav	טַחַב (ז)
to uproot (remove trees or tree stumps)	la'akor	לַעֲקוֹר
to chop down	liχrot	לִכְרוֹת
to deforest (vt)	levare	לְבָרֵא
tree stump	'gedem	גֶּדֶם (ז)
campfire	medura	מְדוּרָה (נ)
forest fire	srefa	שְׂרֵיפָה (נ)
to extinguish (vt)	leχabot	לְכַבּוֹת
forest ranger	ʃomer 'ya'ar	שׁוֹמֵר יַעַר (ז)
protection	ʃmira	שְׁמִירָה (נ)
to protect (~ nature)	liʃmor	לִשְׁמוֹר
poacher	tsayad lelo reʃut	צַיָּיד לְלֹא רְשׁוּת (ז)
steel trap	mal'kodet	מַלְכּוֹדֶת (נ)
to gather, to pick (vt)	lelaket	לְלַקֵּט
to lose one's way	lit'ot	לִתְעוֹת

84. Natural resources

natural resources	otsarot 'teva	אוֹצְרוֹת טֶבַע (ז״ר)
minerals	mine'ralim	מִינֵרָלִים (ז״ר)
deposits	mirbats	מִרְבָּץ (ז)
field (e.g. oilfield)	mirbats	מִרְבָּץ (ז)
to mine (extract)	liχrot	לִכְרוֹת
mining (extraction)	kriya	כְּרִייָה (נ)
ore	afra	עַפְרָה (נ)
mine (e.g. for coal)	miχre	מִכְרֶה (ז)
shaft (mine ~)	pir	פִּיר (ז)
miner	kore	כּוֹרֶה (ז)
gas (natural ~)	gaz	גָּז (ז)
gas pipeline	tsinor gaz	צִינוֹר גָּז (ז)

oil (petroleum)	neft	נֵפְט (ז)
oil pipeline	tsinor neft	צִינוֹר נֵפְט (ז)
oil well	be'er neft	בְּאֵר נֵפְט (נ)
derrick (tower)	migdal ki'duax	מִגְדָּל קִידּוֹחַ (ז)
tanker	meχalit	מֵיכָלִית (נ)

sand	χol	חוֹל (ז)
limestone	'even gir	אֶבֶן גִּיר (נ)
gravel	χatsats	חָצָץ (ז)
peat	kavul	כָּבוּל (ז)
clay	tit	טִיט (ז)
coal	peχam	פֶּחָם (ז)

iron (ore)	barzel	בַּרְזֶל (ז)
gold	zahav	זָהָב (ז)
silver	'kesef	כֶּסֶף (ז)
nickel	'nikel	נִיקֶל (ז)
copper	ne'χoʃet	נְחוֹשֶׁת (נ)

zinc	avats	אָבָץ (ז)
manganese	mangan	מַנְגָּן (ז)
mercury	kaspit	כַּסְפִּית (נ)
lead	o'feret	עוֹפֶרֶת (נ)

mineral	mineral	מִינְרָל (ז)
crystal	gaviʃ	גָּבִישׁ (ז)
marble	'ʃayiʃ	שַׁיִשׁ (ז)
uranium	u'ranyum	אוּרָנִיוּם (ז)

85. Weather

weather	'mezeg avir	מֶזֶג אֲוִויר (ז)
weather forecast	taχazit 'mezeg ha'avir	תַּחֲזִית מֶזֶג הָאֲוִויר (נ)
temperature	tempera'tura	טֶמְפֶּרָטוּרָה (נ)
thermometer	madχom	מַדְחוֹם (ז)
barometer	ba'rometer	בָּרוֹמֶטֶר (ז)

humid (adj)	laχ	לַח
humidity	laχut	לַחוּת (נ)
heat (extreme ~)	χom	חוֹם (ז)
hot (torrid)	χam	חַם
it's hot	χam	חַם

| it's warm | χamim | חָמִים |
| warm (moderately hot) | χamim | חָמִים |

| it's cold | kar | קַר |
| cold (adj) | kar | קַר |

sun	'ʃemeʃ	שֶׁמֶשׁ (נ)
to shine (vi)	lizhor	לִזְהוֹר
sunny (day)	ʃimʃi	שִׁמְשִׁי
to come up (vi)	liz'roaχ	לִזְרוֹחַ
to set (vi)	liʃ'koʽa	לִשְׁקוֹעַ

cloud	anan	עָנָן (ז)
cloudy (adj)	me'unan	מְעוּנָן
rain cloud	av	עָב (ז)
somber (gloomy)	sagriri	סַגְרִירִי
rain	'geʃem	גֶשֶם (ז)
it's raining	yored 'geʃem	יוֹרֵד גֶשֶם
rainy (~ day, weather)	gaʃum	גָשוּם
to drizzle (vi)	letaftef	לְטַפְטֵף
pouring rain	matar	מָטָר (ז)
downpour	mabul	מַבּוּל (ז)
heavy (e.g. ~ rain)	χazak	חָזָק
puddle	ʃlulit	שלוּלִית (נ)
to get wet (in rain)	lehitratev	לְהִתְרַטֵב
fog (mist)	arapel	עֲרָפֶל (ז)
foggy	me'urpal	מְעוּרְפָּל
snow	'ʃeleg	שֶלֶג (ז)
it's snowing	yored 'ʃeleg	יוֹרֵד שֶלֶג

86. Severe weather. Natural disasters

thunderstorm	sufat re'amim	סוּפַת רְעָמִים (נ)
lightning (~ strike)	barak	בָּרָק (ז)
to flash (vi)	livhok	לִבהוֹק
thunder	'ra'am	רַעַם (ז)
to thunder (vi)	lir'om	לִרעוֹם
it's thundering	lir'om	לִרעוֹם
hail	barad	בָּרָד (ז)
it's hailing	yored barad	יוֹרֵד בָּרָד
to flood (vt)	lehatsif	לְהָצִיף
flood, inundation	ʃitafon	שִיטָפוֹן (ז)
earthquake	re'idat adama	רְעִידַת אֲדָמָה (נ)
tremor, shoke	re'ida	רְעִידָה (נ)
epicentre	moked	מוֹקֵד (ז)
eruption	hitpartsut	הִתפָּרְצוּת (נ)
lava	'lava	לָאבָה (נ)
twister	hurikan	הוֹרִיקָן (ז)
tornado	tor'nado	טוֹרנָדוֹ (ז)
typhoon	taifun	טַייפוּן (ז)
hurricane	hurikan	הוֹרִיקָן (ז)
storm	sufa	סוּפָה (נ)
tsunami	tsu'nami	צוּנָאמִי (ז)
cyclone	tsiklon	צִיקלוֹן (ז)
bad weather	sagrir	סַגרִיר (ז)

fire (accident)	srefa	שְׂרֵיפָה (נ)
disaster	ason	אָסוֹן (ז)
meteorite	mete'orit	מֶטְאוֹרִיט (ז)
avalanche	ma'polet ʃlagim	מַפּוֹלֶת שְׁלָגִים (נ)
snowslide	ma'polet ʃlagim	מַפּוֹלֶת שְׁלָגִים (נ)
blizzard	sufat ʃlagim	סוּפַת שְׁלָגִים (נ)
snowstorm	sufat ʃlagim	סוּפַת שְׁלָגִים (נ)

FAUNA

87. Mammals. Predators

predator	χayat 'teref	חַיַּת טֶרֶף (נ)
tiger	'tigris	טִיגְרִיס (ז)
lion	arye	אַרְיֵה (ז)
wolf	ze'ev	זְאֵב (ז)
fox	ʃu'al	שׁוּעָל (ז)
jaguar	yagu'ar	יָגוּאָר (ז)
leopard	namer	נָמֵר (ז)
cheetah	bardelas	בַּרְדְּלָס (ז)
black panther	panter	פַּנְתֵּר (ז)
puma	'puma	פּוּמָה (נ)
snow leopard	namer 'ʃeleg	נָמֵר שֶׁלֶג (ז)
lynx	ʃunar	שׁוּנָר (ז)
coyote	ze'ev ha'aravot	זְאֵב הָעֲרָבוֹת (ז)
jackal	tan	תַּן (ז)
hyena	ʦa'vo'a	צָבוֹעַ (ז)

88. Wild animals

animal	'ba'al χayim	בַּעַל חַיִּים (ז)
beast (animal)	χaya	חַיָּה (נ)
squirrel	sna'i	סְנָאִי (ז)
hedgehog	kipod	קִיפּוֹד (ז)
hare	arnav	אַרְנָב (ז)
rabbit	ʃafan	שָׁפָן (ז)
badger	girit	גִּירִית (נ)
raccoon	dvivon	דְּבִיבוֹן (ז)
hamster	oger	אוֹגֵר (ז)
marmot	mar'mita	מַרְמִיטָה (נ)
mole	χafar'peret	חֲפַרְפֶּרֶת (נ)
mouse	aχbar	עַכְבָּר (ז)
rat	χulda	חוּלְדָה (נ)
bat	atalef	עֲטַלֵּף (ז)
ermine	hermin	הֶרְמִין (ז)
sable	ʦobel	צוֹבֶּל (ז)
marten	dalak	דָּלָק (ז)
weasel	χamus	חָמוּס (ז)
mink	χorfan	חוֹרְפָן (ז)

| beaver | bone | בּוֹנֶה (ז) |
| otter | lutra | לוּטְרָה (נ) |

horse	sus	סוּס (ז)
moose	ayal hakore	אַיָּל הַקּוֹרֵא (ז)
deer	ayal	אַיָּל (ז)
camel	gamal	גָּמָל (ז)

bison	bizon	בִּיזוֹן (ז)
wisent	bizon ei'ropi	בִּיזוֹן אֵירוֹפִּי (ז)
buffalo	te'o	תְּאוֹ (ז)

zebra	'zebra	זֶבְּרָה (נ)
antelope	anti'lopa	אַנְטִילוֹפָּה (ז)
roe deer	ayal hakarmel	אַיָּל הַכַּרְמֶל (ז)
fallow deer	yaχmur	יַחְמוּר (ז)
chamois	ya'el	יָעֵל (ז)
wild boar	χazir bar	חֲזִיר בַּר (ז)

whale	livyatan	לִוְויָתָן (ז)
seal	'kelev yam	כֶּלֶב יָם (ז)
walrus	sus yam	סוּס יָם (ז)
fur seal	dov yam	דּוֹב יָם (ז)
dolphin	dolfin	דּוֹלְפִין (ז)

bear	dov	דּוֹב (ז)
polar bear	dov 'kotev	דּוֹב קוֹטֶב (ז)
panda	'panda	פַּנְדָה (נ)

monkey	kof	קוֹף (ז)
chimpanzee	ʃimpanze	שִׁימְפַּנְזָה (נ)
orangutan	orang utan	אוֹרַנְג-אוּטַן (ז)
gorilla	go'rila	גּוֹרִילָה (נ)
macaque	makak	מָקָק (ז)
gibbon	gibon	גִּיבּוֹן (ז)

elephant	pil	פִּיל (ז)
rhinoceros	karnaf	קַרְנַף (ז)
giraffe	dʒi'rafa	גִּ'ירָפָּה (נ)
hippopotamus	hipopotam	הִיפּוֹפּוֹטָם (ז)

| kangaroo | 'kenguru | קֶנְגּוּרוּ (ז) |
| koala (bear) | ko''ala | קוֹאָלָה (ז) |

mongoose	nemiya	נְמִייָה (נ)
chinchilla	tʃin'tʃila	צִ'ינְצִ'ילָה (נ)
skunk	bo'eʃ	בּוֹאֵשׁ (ז)
porcupine	darban	דַּרְבָּן (ז)

89. Domestic animals

cat	χatula	חֲתוּלָה (נ)
tomcat	χatul	חָתוּל (ז)
dog	'kelev	כֶּלֶב (ז)

horse	sus	סוס (ז)
stallion (male horse)	sus harba'a	סוס הַרבָּעָה (ז)
mare	susa	סוּסָה (נ)
cow	para	פָּרָה (נ)
bull	ʃor	שׁוֹר (ז)
ox	ʃor	שׁוֹר (ז)
sheep (ewe)	kivsa	כִּבשָׂה (נ)
ram	'ayil	אַיִל (ז)
goat	ez	עֵז (נ)
billy goat, he-goat	'tayiʃ	תַּיִש (ז)
donkey	xamor	חֲמוֹר (ז)
mule	'pered	פֶּרֶד (ז)
pig	xazir	חֲזִיר (ז)
piglet	xazarzir	חֲזַרזִיר (ז)
rabbit	arnav	אַרנָב (ז)
hen (chicken)	tarne'golet	תַּרנְגוֹלֶת (נ)
cock	tarnegol	תַּרנְגוֹל (ז)
duck	barvaz	בַּרוָז (ז)
drake	barvaz	בַּרוָז (ז)
goose	avaz	אַוָז (ז)
tom turkey, gobbler	tarnegol 'hodu	תַּרנְגוֹל הוֹדוּ (ז)
turkey (hen)	tarne'golet 'hodu	תַּרנְגוֹלֶת הוֹדוּ (נ)
domestic animals	xayot 'bayit	חַיוֹת בַּיִת (נ"ר)
tame (e.g. ~ hamster)	mevuyat	מְבוּיָת
to tame (vt)	levayet	לְבַיֵית
to breed (vt)	lehar'bi'a	לְהַרבִּיעַ
farm	xava	חַוָוה (נ)
poultry	ofot 'bayit	עוֹפוֹת בַּיִת (נ"ר)
cattle	bakar	בָּקָר (ז)
herd (cattle)	'eder	עֵדֶר (ז)
stable	urva	אוּרוָה (נ)
pigsty	dir xazirim	דִיר חֲזִירִים (ז)
cowshed	'refet	רֶפֶת (נ)
rabbit hutch	arnaviya	אַרנָבִייָה (נ)
hen house	lul	לוּל (ז)

90. Birds

bird	tsipor	צִיפּוֹר (נ)
pigeon	yona	יוֹנָה (נ)
sparrow	dror	דרוֹר (ז)
tit (great tit)	yargazi	יַרגָזִי (ז)
magpie	orev nexalim	עוֹרֵב נְחָלִים (ז)
raven	orev ʃaxor	עוֹרֵב שָׁחוֹר (ז)

crow	orev afor	עוֹרֵב אָפֹר (ז)
jackdaw	ka`ak	קָאָק (ז)
rook	orev hamizra	עוֹרֵב הַמִּזְרָע (ז)
duck	barvaz	בַּרְוָז (ז)
goose	avaz	אַוָז (ז)
pheasant	pasyon	פַּסְיוֹן (ז)
eagle	'ayit	עַיִט (ז)
hawk	neʦ	נֵץ (ז)
falcon	baz	בַּז (ז)
vulture	ozniya	עוֹזְנִיָּה (ז)
condor (Andean ~)	kondor	קוֹנְדוֹר (ז)
swan	barbur	בַּרְבּוּר (ז)
crane	agur	עָגוּר (ז)
stork	χasida	חֲסִידָה (נ)
parrot	'tuki	תּוּכִּי (ז)
hummingbird	ko'libri	קוֹלִיבְּרִי (ז)
peacock	tavas	טַוָּס (ז)
ostrich	bat ya'ana	בַּת יַעֲנָה (נ)
heron	anafa	אֲנָפָה (נ)
flamingo	fla'mingo	פְלָמִינְגוֹ (ז)
pelican	saknai	שַׂקְנַאי (ז)
nightingale	zamir	זָמִיר (ז)
swallow	snunit	סְנוּנִית (נ)
thrush	kiχli	קִיכְלִי (ז)
song thrush	kiχli mezamer	קִיכְלִי מְזַמֵּר (ז)
blackbird	kiχli ʃaχor	קִיכְלִי שָׁחוֹר (ז)
swift	sis	סִיס (ז)
lark	efroni	עֶפְרוֹנִי (ז)
quail	slav	שְׂלָיו (ז)
woodpecker	'neker	נַקָּר (ז)
cuckoo	kukiya	קוּקִיָּה (נ)
owl	yanʃuf	יַנְשׁוּף (ז)
eagle owl	'oaχ	אֹחַ (ז)
wood grouse	seχvi 'ya'ar	שְׂכְוִי יַעַר (ז)
black grouse	seχvi	שְׂכְוִי (ז)
partridge	χogla	חוֹגְלָה (נ)
starling	zarzir	זַרְזִיר (ז)
canary	ka'narit	קָנָרִית (נ)
hazel grouse	seχvi haya'arot	שְׂכְוִי הַיְעָרוֹת (ז)
chaffinch	paroʃ	פָּרוּשׁ (ז)
bullfinch	admonit	אַדְמוֹנִית (נ)
seagull	'ʃaχaf	שַׁחַף (ז)
albatross	albatros	אַלְבַּטְרוֹס (ז)
penguin	pingvin	פִּינְגּוִין (ז)

91. Fish. Marine animals

bream	avroma	אַברוֹמָה (נ)
carp	karpiyon	קַרְפִּיוֹן (ז)
perch	'okunus	אוֹקוּנוּס (ז)
catfish	sfamnun	שְׂפַמְנוּן (ז)
pike	ze'ev 'mayim	זְאֵב מַיִם (ז)

| salmon | 'salmon | סַלְמוֹן (ז) |
| sturgeon | χidkan | חִדְקָן (ז) |

herring	ma'liaχ	מָלִיחַ (ז)
Atlantic salmon	iltit	אִילְתִּית (נ)
mackerel	makarel	מָקָרֵל (ז)
flatfish	dag moʃe ra'benu	דַג מֹשֶׁה רַבֵּנוּ (ז)

zander, pike perch	amnun	אַמְנוּן (ז)
cod	ʃibut	שִׁיבּוּט (ז)
tuna	'tuna	טוּנָה (נ)
trout	forel	פּוֹרֶל (ז)

eel	tslofaχ	צְלוֹפַח (ז)
electric ray	trisanit	תְּרִיסָנִית (נ)
moray eel	mo'rena	מוֹרֶנָה (נ)
piranha	pi'ranya	פִּירַנְיָה (נ)

shark	kariʃ	כָּרִישׁ (ז)
dolphin	dolfin	דוֹלְפִין (ז)
whale	livyatan	לִוְיָתָן (ז)

crab	sartan	סַרְטָן (ז)
jellyfish	me'duza	מֶדוּזָה (נ)
octopus	tamnun	תַמְנוּן (ז)

starfish	koχav yam	כּוֹכַב יָם (ז)
sea urchin	kipod yam	קִיפּוֹד יָם (ז)
seahorse	suson yam	סוּסוֹן יָם (ז)

oyster	tsidpa	צְדָפָה (נ)
prawn	χasilon	חֲסִילוֹן (ז)
lobster	'lobster	לוֹבּסְטֶר (ז)
spiny lobster	'lobster kotsani	לוֹבּסְטֶר קוֹצָנִי (ז)

92. Amphibians. Reptiles

| snake | naχaʃ | נָחָשׁ (ז) |
| venomous (snake) | arsi | אַרְסִי |

viper	'tsefa	צֶפַע (ז)
cobra	'peten	פֶּתֶן (ז)
python	piton	פִּיתוֹן (ז)
boa	χanak	חֲנָק (ז)
grass snake	naχaʃ 'mayim	נָחָשׁ מַיִם (ז)

rattle snake	ʃfifon	שְׁפִיפוֹן (ז)
anaconda	ana'konda	אֲנָקוֹנְדָה (נ)
lizard	leta'a	לְטָאָה (נ)
iguana	igu''ana	אִיגוּאָנָה (נ)
monitor lizard	'koaχ	כֹּחַ (ז)
salamander	sala'mandra	סָלָמַנְדְרָה (נ)
chameleon	zikit	זִיקִית (נ)
scorpion	akrav	עַקְרָב (ז)
turtle	tsav	צָב (ז)
frog	tsfar'deʿa	צְפַרְדֵּעַ (נ)
toad	karpada	קַרְפָּדָה (נ)
crocodile	tanin	תַּנִּין (ז)

93. Insects

insect	χarak	חָרָק (ז)
butterfly	parpar	פַּרְפָּר (ז)
ant	nemala	נְמָלָה (נ)
fly	zvuv	זְבוּב (ז)
mosquito	yatuʃ	יַתּוּשׁ (ז)
beetle	χipuʃit	חִיפּוּשִׁית (נ)
wasp	tsirʿa	צִרְעָה (נ)
bee	dvora	דְּבוֹרָה (נ)
bumblebee	dabur	דַּבּוּר (ז)
gadfly (botfly)	zvuv hasus	זְבוּב הַסּוּס (ז)
spider	akaviʃ	עַכָּבִישׁ (ז)
spider's web	kurei akaviʃ	קוּרֵי עַכָּבִישׁ (ז"ר)
dragonfly	ʃapirit	שַׁפִּירִית (נ)
grasshopper	χagav	חָגָב (ז)
moth (night butterfly)	aʃ	עָשׁ (ז)
cockroach	makak	מַקָּק (ז)
tick	kartsiya	קַרְצִיָּה (נ)
flea	parʿoʃ	פַּרְעֹשׁ (ז)
midge	yavχuʃ	יַבְחוּשׁ (ז)
locust	arbe	אַרְבֶּה (ז)
snail	χilazon	חִלָּזוֹן (ז)
cricket	tsartsar	צְרָצַר (ז)
firefly	gaχlilit	גַחְלִילִית (נ)
ladybird	parat moʃe ra'benu	פָּרַת מֹשֶׁה רַבֵּנוּ (נ)
cockchafer	χipuʃit aviv	חִיפּוּשִׁית אָבִיב (נ)
leech	aluka	עֲלוּקָה (נ)
caterpillar	zaχal	זַחַל (ז)
earthworm	to'laʿat	תּוֹלַעַת (נ)
larva	'deren	דֶּרֶן (ז)

FLORA

tree	ets	עֵץ (ז)
deciduous (adj)	naʃir	נָשִׁיר
coniferous (adj)	maxtani	מַחְטָנִי
evergreen (adj)	yarok ad	יָרוֹק עַד

apple tree	taˈpuax	תַּפּוּחַ (ז)
pear tree	agas	אַגָּס (ז)
sweet cherry tree	gudgedan	גוּדְגְּדָן (ז)
sour cherry tree	duvdevan	דּוּבְדְּבָן (ז)
plum tree	ʃezif	שְׁזִיף (ז)

birch	ʃadar	שָׁדָר (ז)
oak	alon	אַלּוֹן (ז)
linden tree	ˈtilya	טִילְיָה (נ)
aspen	aspa	אַסְפָּה (נ)
maple	ˈeder	אֶדֶר (ז)
spruce	aˈʃuax	אַשּׁוּחַ (ז)
pine	ˈoren	אוֹרֶן (ז)
larch	arzit	אַרְזִית (נ)
fir tree	aˈʃuax	אַשּׁוּחַ (ז)
cedar	ˈerez	אֶרֶז (ז)

poplar	tsaftsefa	צַפְצָפָה (נ)
rowan	ben xuzrar	בֶּן־חֻזְרָר (ז)
willow	arava	עֲרָבָה (נ)
alder	alnus	אַלְנוּס (ז)
beech	aʃur	אָשׁוּר (ז)
elm	buˈkitsa	בּוּקִיצָה (נ)
ash (tree)	mela	מֵילָה (נ)
chestnut	armon	עַרְמוֹן (ז)

magnolia	magˈnolya	מַגְנוֹלְיָה (נ)
palm tree	ˈdekel	דֶּקֶל (ז)
cypress	broʃ	בְּרוֹשׁ (ז)

mangrove	mangrov	מַנְגְּרוֹב (ז)
baobab	baˈobab	בָּאוֹבָּב (ז)
eucalyptus	eikaˈliptus	אֵיקָלִיפְּטוּס (ז)
sequoia	sekˈvoya	סֶקְווֹיָה (נ)

| bush | ˈsiax | שִׂיחַ (ז) |
| shrub | ˈsiax | שִׂיחַ (ז) |

grapevine	'gefen	גֶּפֶן (ז)
vineyard	'kerem	כֶּרֶם (ז)
raspberry bush	'petel	פֶּטֶל (ז)
blackcurrant bush	'siaχ dumdemaniyot ʃχorot	שִׂיחַ דּוּמְדְּמָנִיּוֹת שְׁחוֹרוֹת (ז)
redcurrant bush	'siaχ dumdemaniyot adumot	שִׂיחַ דּוּמְדְּמָנִיּוֹת אֲדוּמּוֹת (ז)
gooseberry bush	χazarzar	חֲזַרְזַר (ז)
acacia	ʃita	שִׁיטָה (נ)
barberry	berberis	בֶּרְבֶּרִיס (ז)
jasmine	yasmin	יַסְמִין (ז)
juniper	ar'ar	עַרְעָר (ז)
rosebush	'siaχ vradim	שִׂיחַ וְרָדִים (ז)
dog rose	'vered bar	וֶרֶד בָּר (ז)

96. Fruits. Berries

fruit	pri	פְּרִי (ז)
fruits	perot	פֵּירוֹת (ז"ר)
apple	ta'puaχ	תַּפּוּחַ (ז)
pear	agas	אַגָּס (ז)
plum	ʃezif	שְׁזִיף (ז)
strawberry (garden ~)	tut sade	תּוּת שָׂדֶה (ז)
sour cherry	duvdevan	דּוּבְדְּבָן (ז)
sweet cherry	gudgedan	גּוּדְגְּדָן (ז)
grape	anavim	עֲנָבִים (ז"ר)
raspberry	'petel	פֶּטֶל (ז)
blackcurrant	dumdemanit ʃχora	דּוּמְדְּמָנִית שְׁחוֹרָה (נ)
redcurrant	dumdemanit aduma	דּוּמְדְּמָנִית אֲדוּמָּה (נ)
gooseberry	χazarzar	חֲזַרְזַר (ז)
cranberry	χamutsit	חֲמוּצִית (נ)
orange	tapuz	תַּפּוּז (ז)
tangerine	klemen'tina	קְלֶמֶנְטִינָה (נ)
pineapple	'ananas	אֲנָנָס (ז)
banana	ba'nana	בַּנָנָה (נ)
date	tamar	תָּמָר (ז)
lemon	limon	לִימוֹן (ז)
apricot	'miʃmeʃ	מִשְׁמֵשׁ (ז)
peach	afarsek	אֲפַרְסֵק (ז)
kiwi	'kivi	קִיוִוי (ז)
grapefruit	eʃkolit	אֶשְׁכּוֹלִית (נ)
berry	garger	גַּרְגַּר (ז)
berries	gargerim	גַּרְגְּרִים (ז"ר)
cowberry	uχmanit aduma	אוּכְמָנִית אֲדוּמָּה (נ)
wild strawberry	tut 'ya'ar	תּוּת יַעַר (ז)
bilberry	uχmanit	אוּכְמָנִית (נ)

97. Flowers. Plants

flower	'peraχ	פֶּרַח (ז)
bouquet (of flowers)	zer	זֵר (ז)
rose (flower)	'vered	וֶרֶד (ז)
tulip	tsiv'oni	צִבְעוֹנִי (ז)
carnation	tsi'poren	צִיפּוֹרֶן (ז)
gladiolus	glad'yola	גְלַדְיוֹלָה (נ)
cornflower	dganit	דְגָנִית (נ)
harebell	pa'amonit	פַּעֲמוֹנִית (נ)
dandelion	ʃinan	שִׁינָן (ז)
camomile	kamomil	קָמוֹמִיל (ז)
aloe	alvai	אַלְוַי (ז)
cactus	'kaktus	קַקְטוּס (ז)
rubber plant, ficus	'fikus	פִיקוּס (ז)
lily	ʃoʃana	שׁוֹשַׁנָה (נ)
geranium	ge'ranyum	גֶרַנְיוּם (ז)
hyacinth	yakinton	יָקִינְטוֹן (ז)
mimosa	mi'moza	מִימוֹזָה (נ)
narcissus	narkis	נַרְקִיס (ז)
nasturtium	'kova hanazir	כּוֹבַע הַנָזִיר (ז)
orchid	saχlav	סַחְלָב (ז)
peony	admonit	אַדְמוֹנִית (נ)
violet	sigalit	סִיגָלִית (נ)
pansy	amnon vetamar	אַמְנוֹן וְתָמָר (ז)
forget-me-not	ziχ'rini	זִכְרִינִי (ז)
daisy	marganit	מַרְגָנִית (נ)
poppy	'pereg	פֶּרֶג (ז)
hemp	ka'nabis	קָנַאבִּיס (ז)
mint	'menta	מֶנְתָה (נ)
lily of the valley	zivanit	זִיוָנִית (נ)
snowdrop	ga'lantus	גָלַנְטוּס (ז)
nettle	sirpad	סִרְפָּד (ז)
sorrel	χum'a	חוּמְעָה (נ)
water lily	nufar	נוּפָר (ז)
fern	ʃaraχ	שְׁרָךְ (ז)
lichen	χazazit	חֲזָזִית (נ)
conservatory (greenhouse)	χamama	חֲמָמָה (נ)
lawn	midʃa'a	מִדְשָׁאָה (נ)
flowerbed	arugat praχim	עֲרוּגַת פְּרָחִים (נ)
plant	'tsemaχ	צֶמַח (ז)
grass	'deʃe	דֶשֶׁא (ז)
blade of grass	giv'ol 'esev	גִבְעוֹל עֵשֶׂב (ז)

leaf	ale	עָלֶה (ז)
petal	ale ko'teret	עָלֶה כּוֹתֶרֶת (ז)
stem	giv'ol	גִּבְעוֹל (ז)
tuber	'pka'at	פְּקַעַת (נ)
young plant (shoot)	'nevet	נֶבֶט (ז)
thorn	kots	קוֹץ (ז)
to blossom (vi)	lif'roaχ	לִפְרוֹחַ
to fade, to wither	linbol	לִנְבּוֹל
smell (odour)	'reaχ	רֵיחַ (ז)
to cut (flowers)	ligzom	לִגְזוֹם
to pick (a flower)	liktof	לִקְטוֹף

98. Cereals, grains

grain	tvu'a	תְּבוּאָה (נ)
cereal crops	dganim	דְּגָנִים (ז"ר)
ear (of barley, etc.)	ʃi'bolet	שִׁיבּוֹלֶת (נ)
wheat	χita	חִיטָה (נ)
rye	ʃifon	שִׁיפּוֹן (ז)
oats	ʃi'bolet ʃu'al	שִׁיבּוֹלֶת שׁוּעָל (נ)
millet	'doχan	דּוֹחַן (ז)
barley	se'ora	שְׂעוֹרָה (נ)
maize	'tiras	תִּירָס (ז)
rice	'orez	אוֹרֶז (ז)
buckwheat	ku'semet	כּוּסֶמֶת (נ)
pea plant	afuna	אֲפוּנָה (נ)
kidney bean	ʃu'it	שְׁעוּעִית (נ)
soya	'soya	סוֹיָה (נ)
lentil	adaʃim	עֲדָשִׁים (נ"ר)
beans (pulse crops)	pol	פּוֹל (ז)

COUNTRIES OF THE WORLD

99. Countries. Part 1

Afghanistan	afganistan	אַפְגָּנִיסְטָן (נ)
Albania	al'banya	אַלְבַּנְיָה (נ)
Argentina	argen'tina	אַרְגֶּנְטִינָה (נ)
Armenia	ar'menya	אַרְמֶנְיָה (נ)
Australia	ost'ralya	אוֹסְטְרַלְיָה (נ)
Austria	'ostriya	אוֹסְטְרְיָה (נ)
Azerbaijan	azerbaidʒan	אָזֶרְבַּייגָ'ן (נ)
The Bahamas	iyey ba'hama	אִיֵי בָּהָאמָה (ז"ר)
Bangladesh	bangladeʃ	בַּנְגְלָדֶשׁ (נ)
Belarus	'belarus	בֶּלָרוּס (נ)
Belgium	'belgya	בֶּלְגְיָה (נ)
Bolivia	bo'livya	בּוֹלִיבְיָה (נ)
Bosnia and Herzegovina	'bosniya	בּוֹסְנְיָה (נ)
Brazil	brazil	בְּרָזִיל (נ)
Bulgaria	bul'garya	בּוּלְגַּרְיָה (נ)
Cambodia	kam'bodya	קַמְבּוֹדְיָה (נ)
Canada	'kanada	קָנָדָה (נ)
Chile	'tʃile	צִ'ילֶה (נ)
China	sin	סִין (נ)
Colombia	ko'lombya	קוֹלוֹמְבְּיָה (נ)
Croatia	kro"atya	קְרוֹאַטְיָה (נ)
Cuba	'kuba	קוּבָּה (נ)
Cyprus	kafrisin	קַפְרִיסִין (נ)
Czech Republic	'tʃeχya	צֶ'כְיָה (נ)
Denmark	'denemark	דֶּנֶמֶרְק (נ)
Dominican Republic	hare'publika hadomeni'kanit	הָרֶפּוּבְּלִיקָה הַדּוֹמִינִיקָנִית (נ)
Ecuador	ekvador	אֶקְוָדוֹר (נ)
Egypt	mits'rayim	מִצְרַיִם (נ)
England	'angliya	אַנְגְלְיָה (נ)
Estonia	es'tonya	אֶסְטוֹנְיָה (נ)
Finland	'finland	פִינְלַנְד (נ)
France	tsarfat	צָרְפַת (נ)
French Polynesia	poli'nezya hatsarfatit	פּוֹלִינֶזְיָה הַצָּרְפָתִית (נ)
Georgia	'gruzya	גְּרוּזְיָה (נ)
Germany	ger'manya	גֶּרְמַנְיָה (נ)
Ghana	'gana	גָּאנָה (נ)
Great Britain	bri'tanya hagdola	בְּרִיטַנְיָה הַגְּדוֹלָה (נ)
Greece	yavan	יָוָן (נ)
Haiti	ha"iti	הָאִיטִי (נ)
Hungary	hun'garya	הוּנְגַּרְיָה (נ)

100. Countries. Part 2

Iceland	'island	אִיסלַנד (נ)
India	'hodu	הוֹדוּ (נ)
Indonesia	indo'nezya	אִינדוֹנֶזיָה (נ)
Iran	iran	אִירָן (נ)
Iraq	irak	עִירָאק (נ)
Ireland	'irland	אִירלַנד (נ)
Israel	yisra'el	יִשֹרָאֵל (נ)
Italy	i'talya	אִיטַליָה (נ)

Jamaica	dʒa'maika	ג'מַייקָה (נ)
Japan	yapan	יָפָן (נ)
Jordan	yarden	יַרדֵן (נ)
Kazakhstan	kazaχstan	קָזַחסטָן (נ)
Kenya	'kenya	קֶניָה (נ)
Kirghizia	kirgizstan	קִירגִיזסטָן (נ)
Kuwait	kuveit	כּוּוֵית (נ)

Laos	la'os	לָאוֹס (נ)
Latvia	'latviya	לָטבִיָה (נ)
Lebanon	levanon	לְבָנוֹן (נ)
Libya	luv	לוּב (נ)
Liechtenstein	liχtenʃtain	לִיכטֶנשטַיין (נ)
Lithuania	'lita	לִיטָא (נ)
Luxembourg	luksemburg	לוּקסֶמבּוּרג (נ)

North Macedonia	make'donya	מָקֵדוֹניָה (נ)
Madagascar	madagaskar	מָדָגַסקָר (ז)
Malaysia	ma'lezya	מָלֶזיָה (נ)
Malta	'malta	מַלטָה (נ)
Mexico	'meksiko	מֶקסִיקוֹ (נ)

Moldova, Moldavia	mol'davya	מוֹלדַבִיָה (נ)
Monaco	mo'nako	מוֹנָקוֹ (נ)
Mongolia	mon'golya	מוֹנגוֹליָה (נ)
Montenegro	monte'negro	מוֹנטֶנֶגרוֹ (נ)
Morocco	ma'roko	מָרוֹקוֹ (נ)
Myanmar	miyanmar	מְיַאנמָר (נ)

Namibia	na'mibya	נָמִיבִּיָה (נ)
Nepal	nepal	נֶפָּאל (נ)
Netherlands	'holand	הוֹלַנד (נ)
New Zealand	nyu 'ziland	נִיוּ זִילַנד (נ)
North Korea	ko'rei'a hatsfonit	קוֹרֵיאָה הַצפוֹנִית (נ)
Norway	nor'vegya	נוֹרבֶגִיָה (נ)

101. Countries. Part 3

Pakistan	pakistan	פָּקִיסטָן (נ)
Palestine	falastin	פָּלֶסטִין (נ)
Panama	pa'nama	פָּנָמָה (נ)
Paraguay	paragvai	פָּרָגווַאי (נ)

Peru	peru	פֵּרוּ (נ)
Poland	polin	פּוֹלִין (נ)
Portugal	portugal	פּוֹרטוּגָל (נ)
Romania	ro'manya	רוֹמַניָה (נ)
Russia	'rusya	רוֹסיָה (נ)

Saudi Arabia	arav hasa'udit	עֲרָב הַסָעוּדִית (נ)
Scotland	'skotland	סקוֹטלָנד (נ)
Senegal	senegal	סֶנֶגָל (נ)
Serbia	'serbya	סֶרבִּיָה (נ)
Slovakia	slo'vakya	סלוֹבָקיָה (נ)
Slovenia	slo'venya	סלוֹבֶניָה (נ)

South Africa	drom 'afrika	דרוֹם אַפרִיקָה (נ)
South Korea	ko'rei'a hadromit	קוֹרֵיאָה הַדרוֹמִית (נ)
Spain	sfarad	סְפָרַד (נ)
Suriname	surinam	סוּרִינָאם (נ)
Sweden	'ʃvedya	שבֶדיָה (נ)
Switzerland	'ʃvaits	שוַויץ (נ)
Syria	'surya	סוּריָה (נ)

Taiwan	taivan	טַייוָון (נ)
Tajikistan	tadʒikistan	טָגֵ'יקיסטָן (נ)
Tanzania	tan'zanya	טַנזָניָה (נ)
Tasmania	tas'manya	טַסמַניָה (נ)
Thailand	'tailand	תַאילַנד (נ)
Tunisia	tu'nisya	טוּנִיסיָה (נ)
Turkey	'turkiya	טוּרקִיָה (נ)
Turkmenistan	turkmenistan	טוּרקמֶנִיסטָן (נ)

Ukraine	uk'rayna	אוֹקרַאינָה (נ)
United Arab Emirates	iχud ha'emi'royot ha'araviyot	אִיחוּד הָאֱמִירוּיוֹת הָעַרָבִיוֹת (ז)
United States of America	artsot habrit	אַרצוֹת הַבּרִית (נ"ר)
Uruguay	urugvai	אוּרוּגוַואי (נ)
Uzbekistan	uzbekistan	אוֹזבֶּקִיסטָן (נ)

Vatican City	vatikan	וָתִיקָן (ז)
Venezuela	venetsu"ela	וֶנֶצוּאֵלָה (נ)
Vietnam	vyetnam	וִייֶטנָאם (נ)
Zanzibar	zanzibar	זָנזִיבָּר (נ)